THE CALVARY STORY

THE CALVARY STORY

How God Transformed a Dying Church of 60 People to a Vibrant Church of 6,000 Followers of Jesus Christ

LARRY DeWITT

Cornerstone Network Association

For information contact:
www.cornerstonenetwork.com
larry_dewitt@yahoo.com

Published by:
Cornerstone Network Association

Cover design by Melissa Carlson
Interior book design by Francine Platt, Eden Graphics, Inc.
Interior photo credit: Davizro

Paperback ISBN 978-1-60645-341-4
Ebook ISBN 978-1-60645-342-1

Library of Congress Number: Pending

Printed in the United States of America

First Edition

Dedications

Daily, I give thanks to God for Rebecca (Beccy), my life partner in Christ. She is joyful, peaceful, prayerful and courageous in believing God will do the amazing.

Thank God for her parents, Strat and Marge Shufelt, who walked and served Christ with giants of the faith:

- **H. A. Ironside**...Dad Shufelt was soloist and choral director at Moody Church, and in crusades throughout the British Isles. Her dad brought the hymn "How Great Thou Art" back to America.
- **A. W. Tozer**...her dad was music director for this well-known Bible teacher and author.
- **Billy Graham**...her dad was his soloist and choral director in crusades for youth in 10+ major cities of Europe after World War II, and then in many USA crusades.

Beccy and her parents helped me catch a larger vision of what God could and would do. She willingly let go of a thriving ministry in a historic church, lovely home, good income and comfortable life to "Go for it!" We moved to California and started all over again with faith and a dream of a fresh way of doing church that would reach a new and changing culture.

It happened...Calvary Community, Westlake Village, California.

The principals shared in this book have been shared with many seminarians and 100's of pastors in the US, and through Linus Morris and Christian Associates in Europe.

Beccy also believed that some day we would launch a Christian high school. Now, with joy, we watch the impact of Oaks Christian...rated as one of the top Christian schools in America.

Thank God for Alice, my mom, who prayed fervently that God would rescue a wayward son, and that he would follow and serve Christ.

Thank God for my dad, Austin, whose dying words to me were,"Serve Christ with all your heart!".

Praise to our Lord Jesus Christ, who has done more to build His Church than we ever saw or imagined!

Peter Wagner was my mentor and the cofounder with Dr. Donald McGavran of the Church Growth Movement in America. Founder of the World Prayer Center.

– Larry DeWitt

March 19, 1990

Rev. Larry DeWitt
The Calvary Community Church
31293 Via Colinas
Thousand Oaks, CA 91362

Dear Larry:

I want to thank you from the depths of my heart for your willingness and that of your staff to meet with my Doctor of Ministry students this winter quarter.

One of my greatest privileges as a professor is to hear the reports these pastors bring back to class after visiting your services and doing the interview. Through the years Calvary Community Church has been a tremendous inspiration to the class—truly life changing for some. I realize that this is a relatively small thing for you, but it is tremendously important for us.

I think I have been negligent in the past in not sending you any copies of the papers the pastors have written on your church. I'll try to start this in the future. Keep in mind that these folks are not professional church consultants, but I'm quite sure that you will be interested in how some outsiders are seeing your church.

For the past dozen years, I have done two Dr. Min. Church Growth I courses each winter, one in February and one in March. Beginning next year, I'm cutting back to one class which will be held the first two weeks of March. This means that my teaching assistant will be phoning your office for one interview next year instead of two, and that the group of pastors who come may be larger.

Thanks again, Larry, for your generosity to us and your fellowship in the gospel.

Warmly,

C. Peter Wagner

Professor of Church Growth

TABLE OF CONTENTS

INTRODUCTION

When did you last say, "It's about time"?

I quickly perused Ecclesiastes 3: "There is a time for everything." I was hoping to find the words, "a time to write a book." Verse 7 came the closest . . . "a time to speak."

In 1976, I led the Calvary Community, a small, traditional church which was terminally ill, through its rebirth. Recently, I reviewed the rebirthing principles and was amazed to find how valid those assumptions were, and still are. Some things change, but many principles are valid generation after generation. My hope is to retrofit these principles for the challenges of the next decade.

PASS IT ON: Praise God for pastors in America who are toughing it out, trusting to see more happen for Christ. While attempting to build churches on the Rock, Christ Jesus, you may feel more like boats—breaking up on the rocks rather than building up; caught in squalls rather than sailing on; tossed about by turbulence rather than staying on course.

I want to speak to you as a pastor who came to a church struggling to survive and believed God for a new start, a new birth. I would like to share lessons learned in the process: the pains, pressures, and privileges of rebirthing a church. It is time to pass on these principles, not as theory, but as assumptions tried and proven by the test of time. I have an increased passion to share what I believe will be practical and helpful for pastors and other leaders of churches that are stuck, not growing, in need of a rebirth. God has already used these lessons, and I believe that, somehow, he will use them for the rebirth of many more churches. My prayer is that, with God's help, I might be able to assist both leaders and their churches in getting on course with a clear sense of direction.

Calvary Community was one of the very first church-growth models in America, and we have been privileged to be a part directly or indirectly in the planting, birthing, or rebirthing of many churches. The Calvary Community Purpose Statement is now in churches all over the world. The Priorities we established have helped many churches regroup and refocus their mission.

One morning, I was reading Psalm 45. This psalm was probably written by a director of music for one of King David's royal weddings.

> *"My heart is stirred by a noble theme as I recite my verses for the king; my tongue is the pen of a skillful writer."* (Ps. 45:1)

The single greatest thing happening in the world today is: Christ is building his Church!

Could there be a more noble theme than this?

> *"'Who do you say I am?'"*
>
> *Simon Peter answered, 'You are the Christ, the Son of the living God.'*

Jesus replied, 'Blessed are you, Simon, son of Jonah, for this was not revealed to you by man, but by my Father in heaven. And I tell you that you are Peter, and on this rock, I will build my church, and the gates of Hades will not overcome it.'" (Matt. 16:15–18)

May those words serve well in the building of his Church.

SECTION A.
PERSONAL LIFE OF A LEADER

"GET A LIFE"

Premise: A healthy church must be led by a healthy pastor, who has developed perspective on his life, and clarified his life purpose.

1

PERSONAL PERSPECTIVE

"Who Am I, Lord?"

God used Nathan the prophet to give King David a piercing perspective on his past: *"I took you from the pasture and from following the flock, to be ruler over my people Israel. I have been with you wherever you have gone."* (1 Chron. 17:7) Then God gave Nathan insight into David's future: *"I will raise up your offspring to succeed you, one of your own sons, and I will establish his kingdom. He is the one who will build a house for me, and I will establish his throne forever."* (vv. 11-12) In response, *"King David went in and sat before the LORD, and he said: 'Who am I, O Lord God, and what is my family, that you have brought me this far?'"* (v. 16)

Forty years later, Solomon, the son of this prophecy and the builder of the Temple, looked back and summarized his own life in perspective:

A. Perspective from Solomon the Wise (Ecclesiastes 3)

1. Recognize the Seasons of Life

"There is a time for everything, and a season for every activity under heaven." (v. 1)

A TIME. One Greek concept of time that we in the Western World relate to is "*chronos*": measuring and keeping track of time. We use chronologies, chronometers, chronographs, etc., to track generations, decades, days, hours, minutes, seconds, and nanoseconds. We watch Olympic competitors win the gold by thousandths of seconds. We live in a chase-the-clock world. This is not the kind of time we see in Ecclesiastes.

Another Greek word for time is "*kairos*," which is comparable to the Hebrew concept "et" or "eth." This is the concept used in Ecclesiastes. It is not as much about measuring time or chronology as it is about valuing time . . . the marking of significant events. Solomon wrote about a time of opportunity, the right time, or an appointed time. His emphasis was not on efficiency—doing things right, but on effectiveness—doing the right things.

A SEASON. We need all the seasons. Which is your favorite? Is one season more beautiful than another to you? It's spring . . . time to plant and see things sprout. It's summer . . . time for warmth and recreation in the sun. It's fall . . . time for color and harvesting. It's winter . . . time for things to die out so that they can be reborn.

I believe Solomon reflected back on his own times and seasons as he wrote Ecclesiastes 3:2–8

> *"There is a time for everything, and a season for every activity under heaven: a time to be born and a time to die, a time to plant and a time to uproot, a time to kill and a time to heal, a time to tear down and a time to build, a time to weep and a time to laugh, a time to mourn and a time to dance, a time to scatter stones and a time to gather them, a time to embrace and a time to refrain, a time to search and a time to give up, a time to keep and a time to throw away, a time to tear and a time to mend, a time to be silent and a time to speak, a time to love and a time to hate, a time for war and a time for peace."*

Like it or not, our lives are made up of seasons. Some welcome us with pleasant breezes, some catch us by storm. Some are in our control, some are beyond our control, some are out of our control; yet we know God is in control. Perspective comes as we recognize the seasons of our lives.

Question: Which of these seasons in Ecclesiastes 3 are you experiencing right now?

2. See the Beauty of the Seasons

Solomon asks, *"What does the worker gain from his toil? I have seen the burden God has laid on men."* (vv. 9-10)

What's the point of it all? Not much, unless you see God's hand in it and through it. *"He has made everything beautiful in its time."* (v. 11) Some times of life are unpleasant or downright ugly; yet the beauty comes in recognizing God's hand in the seasons of our lives. Perspective on our lives comes as we look back and say . . . aha! . . . that winter storm was getting me ready for this spring refreshing . . . that season was part of preparing me for this season.

3. Sense God's Purpose in Life

"He has also set eternity in the hearts of men; yet they cannot fathom what God has done from beginning to end." (v. 11) There is a taste of destiny, a touch of eternity, in the tum of events in life. Do you see God's hand in the times and seasons of life? Caution: if you keep dealing with life only in terms of your "to do" lists and daytimers, your days will lose meaning, your life will lose significance, and you will lose your sense of destiny. Try to see time the way Solomon describes it. There are prime times in your life. There are special seasons God brings to your life. Sensing the purpose of God's chronometer in your life events can change all of time and eternity for you.

I have added a section to my daytimer. Every day, I list the significant God Events that happen. I reflect on my day and ask myself what was really important; where did I experience something that was obviously God's time or opportunity? It's amazing how many entries I can have in just one day when I'm actively looking for what I call "God Stuff."

4. Assume God's Good Intentions for Your Life

"There will be a time for every activity, a time for every deed." (v. 17) Assume that there will be a right time and enough time for everything God wants you to accomplish for him. Assume that the work God wants to produce from your life will happen at the right time, if you are responsive to his timetable. I've stopped talking about "time problems"; what I actually have are perspective problems, priority problems, pacing problems, and planning problems. I have enough time for everything God wants me to do.

This is very affirming, very encouraging.

- Recognize the Seasons of Life
- See the Beauty of the Seasons
- Sense God's Purpose in Life
- Assume God's Good Intentions for Your Life

Perspective is seeing life in terms of God's work in your life. Welcome the seasons; don't fight them. Look for the beauty . . . it's there!

God took his time preparing his servants. I look back and realize that God took almost 20 years to prepare me for the rebirth of Calvary Community.

B. Perspective from My Own Life

"Why?" You've heard little children say it thirty times in a day. "Why me?" You've seen adults express it in actions or attitudes. "Why me, Lord?" can be grounds for a gripe session with God, or an expression of gratitude for God's grace. It's really a great question to ask in gaining perspective on the seasons, times, and events of our lives. *"And we know that in all things God works for the good of those who love him, who have been called according to his purpose."* (Rom. 8:28)

God doesn't cause all things. All things are not good. But we know God brings good out of all things. Just trust his purpose and love him.

When I look at my life in retrospect, two life principles become obvious:

1. **TOUGH TIMES** were followed by **NEW SEASONS**; and God had placed
2. **SIGNIFICANT PEOPLE** in my life to help me learn **LIFE LESSONS** during those seasons.

TOUGH TIMES. I have read birth-order studies, but they don't help me much in understanding myself. I'm child number 7 out of 8. I like to say I came from a tribe rather than a family. As a teenager, I had a very limited sense of my worth, little or no thought about the future, and virtually no sense of hope. The more trouble I got into and the more troubled I became, the more I was annoyed by hearing my mother's prayers of hope for me. She kept praying and hoping for my salvation and for God's purpose for my future.

There were three of us in high school who got into trouble together. One of my buddies is now a blackjack dealer in Las Vegas, and the other committed suicide. I practically failed English in 11th grade, because I couldn't give a speech in front of others. Then, as a senior in high school, on probation as a result of some teenage antics, God brought a new season to my life.

NEW SEASON. A teacher from my home church in Michigan and my pastor's wife (two SIGNIFICANT PEOPLE in my life), asked me if I would be interested in attending Wheaton Academy, the prep school of Wheaton College in Illinois. A Detroit "hood," I found myself a displaced person in a private Christian high school. The reason for my cooperation was to get away from home and escape my troubles, or so I thought. I met Jesus Christ as my Savior within two weeks, and God brought a new season to my life. I began to sense that God loved me, to realize I was worth something to him, to think about my future, and to seek the purpose he had for me.

> *"There is surely a future hope for you."* (Prov. 23:18)
>
> *"'I know the plans I have for you,' declares the* LORD, *'plans to prosper you and not to harm you, plans to give you hope and a future.'"* (Jer. 29:11)

From that day when I found Christ, I've lived with a sense of amazement at God's grace in rescuing me from myself and giving me hope. I now see this as one of the essential lessons to living a healthy life in Christ.

Life Lesson **LIVE LIFE WITH AN ATTITUDE OF GRATITUDE TO GOD**

TOUGH TIMES. College? Who, me? Before meeting Christ, I hadn't even considered it. I attended Wheaton College, majoring in science with plans to be a medical missionary. I thought that would be the greatest thing I could do to show my gratitude to God. Then came major trouble: my father developed cancer. During my last two years of college, many times I wanted to quit and go home; yet I knew that part of my father's hope and motivation to keep going was to see his son finish college and serve the Lord. I took my finals and, instead of participating in my college graduation ceremony, I went home to say goodbye to my father and witness his graduation to heaven on Father's Day. This SIGNIFICANT PERSON's last words to me became a life theme . . .

Life Lesson **IF YOU'RE GOING TO SERVE GOD, SERVE HIM WITH ALL YOUR HEART**

My father's words and his death, the week of my college graduation, became the greatest human motivation in my life. I had been looking forward to spending time with my family after college, particularly my father. But I made the life choice to be better rather than bitter.

Life Lesson **BE BETTER RATHER THAN BITTER**

NEW SEASON. One week after my college graduation and my dad's graduation to heaven, I found myself with an unexpected job: youth pastor at my home church! They asked me because I had attended a Christian college and had some Bible background. I saw this as a transitional time before going on to med school . . . but God grabbed my heart. My focus shifted from medicine to pastoring . . . both help people to be healthy and whole. A brief summer job turned into two years, and through that experience, God affirmed my calling to invest my life in pastoral ministry.

God brought Rebecca and me together. She is God's choice partner for me . . . the most SIGNIFICANT PERSON. She grew up in a ministry home; her father, J. Stratton Shufelt, had invested fifty years of his life traveling in musical evangelism. She brought into our marriage the positive perspective on ministry she had learned from her mother: serving Christ full-time is a privilege. Beccy earned her PHT (Putting Hubby Through) Degree teaching junior high school, while I prepared for pastoring at Fuller Theological Seminary. Sure, pastoral life has its stresses, but we've chosen to view it from a point of blessing, rather than from a point of martyrdom. She helped me to learn this:

Life Lesson **SERVING GOD IS A GREAT PRIVILEGE**

Another **SIGNIFICANT PERSON** was Dr. Malcolm Cronk, my college pastor, who had infused into me excitement about sharing God's Word. He was the pastor who married us, and when we asked him what advice he had for a young couple entering the ministry, he simply said:

Life Lesson **ENCOURAGE PEOPLE**

NEW SEASON. After seminary and five months at the Near East School of Archeological and Biblical Research in Jerusalem, we began the great adventure of pastoring a new church plant in Orangevale, California. I remember my first day as a "Senior Pastor."

After my books were unpacked, I sat down at my desk in my new office, and I realized I didn't have the faintest idea where to start. I searched through my seminary notes in a desperate quest to answer, "What am I supposed to do on my first day as a pastor?" Somehow I had left seminary with the impression that people were going to be knocking at my door asking me critical questions about European theology . . . 33 years later, that still hasn't happened.

There was our neighbor, Mrs. Poster, who bluntly confronted me at the door after the service each Sunday, telling me I had said thus-and-so, and she simply didn't understand what I was talking about! She got the seminary out of me very quickly, and she helped me learn to speak to people where they were, not where I wished they were.

Life Lesson **SPEAK IN WORDS PEOPLE CAN UNDERSTAND**

TOUGH TIMES. Three months after we began pastoring, we were off to a winter youth camp in the Sierras with a few teens. I ended up with an extended stay in the hospital, paralyzed with a broken back as a result of a tobogganing accident. Beccy began to shield the mail from me, because of the doubts expressed by supposedly mature Christians . . . "We don't understand how God could allow this to happen to a young pastor just getting started in his first church," etc. There were weeks of not knowing if I would ever walk again, or if we would ever be able to have children; but the Lord taught us the incredible peace that comes from trusting him. It was a year of living with a full body brace and a great deal of dependence on God. He gave us an important lesson in our boot camp of pastoral training:

Life Lesson TRUST GOD IN THE TOUGH TIMES

I have learned to:

1) accept the TOUGH TIMES of life,
2) watch for SIGNIFICANT PEOPLE,
3) learn LIFE LESSONS, and
4) welcome the NEW SEASONS which follow (they always do!)

Pause, pray, and recognize God's touch of destiny on your life. Assume that all of your tough times, seasons, and essential life lessons are merely preparation for the future God has in mind for you. Believe that there will be time for everything God wants you to do in life.

> *"Be very careful, then, how you live – not as unwise but as wise, making the most of every opportunity."*
> (Eph. 5:15-16)

Healthy Perspective on Past Experience is Essential Preparation for Your Future Ministry

HOW TO ACQUIRE PERSPECTIVE:

Read Ecclesiastes 3 again.

Reflect on and identify the MAJOR SEASONS of your life:

Recall and identify the SIGNIFICANT PEOPLE in your life:

Record the essential LIFE LESSONS learned from these people:

Praise God for these people and their significant contribution to who you are becoming as a leader in Christ.

Consider writing or phoning them, to thank them for being there for you at that season of your life, recognizing the lessons they helped you learn.

2

PERSONAL LIFE PURPOSE

"Why Am I Here, Lord?"

A. Christ Lived With a Clear Sense of Purpose

It was when Jesus was twelve years of age; the year before his Bar Mitzvah, when he would become a full member of the synagogue with rights to read and speak God's Word in public. The family, with many others from Nazareth, had made their annual trek to Jerusalem for the event of the year—the Feast of the Passover. Jesus' parents left for home and discovered he was not traveling with the group from Nazareth. They frantically returned to Jerusalem looking for him. After three days they found him in the Temple Courts sitting with the teachers, both listening and asking questions. His mother did the typical parent thing; she asked, *"Son, why have you treated us like this? Your father and I have been anxiously searching for you."* (Luke 2:48) His response drew a line of distinction between his earthly father and God the Father, and he quickly identified with his Heavenly Father: *"Didn't you know I had to be in my Father's house?"* (v. 49)

Does it strike you as strange that a 12-year-old had this incredible concern for what his Father in heaven was about?

It was twenty years later, when Christ had just launched his public ministry. He was again returning to Nazareth from Jerusalem, by way of Samaria. His hungry disciples returned from town with food and found Jesus having a forbidden conversation with a Samaritan woman. He talked with the disciples about his life purpose, and, in John 4:32,34, Jesus said, "*I have food to eat that you know nothing about. My food is to do the will of him who sent me and to finish his work."*

He clearly communicated to them his appetite to do God the Father's will, his awareness that he was sent, and his determination to finish his life purpose.

It was the second Passover of his ministry, when he had a "like-father, like-son" discussion with his listeners, in John, chapter 5: *"My father is always at his work to this very day, and I, too, am working."* (17) *"For the very work that the Father has given me to finish, and which I am doing, testifies that the Father has sent me."* (36) He talks about his Father nine times in this passage and calls himself the Son ten times.

It was when he was en route to Jerusalem and his Passion that he spoke openly and clearly of his purpose. Salome made the request that her sons, James and John, would sit on Christ's right and left in his glory. His response; *"For even the Son of Man did not come to be served, but to serve, and to give his life as a ransom for many."* (Mark 10:45)

It was the very next day when he invited himself to a private party at the house of Zacchaeus, the chief tax collector of Jericho. After Zacchaeus stood up and openly stated his change of heart and recognition of Christ as Lord, Jesus made a public announcement to all who were present. *"The Son of Man came to seek and to save what was lost."* (Luke 19:10)

It was Thursday evening of Passion Week when Jesus prayed in the Garden his personal passion to his Father: *"I have brought you glory on earth by completing the work you gave me to do. And now, Father, glorify me in your presence with the glory I had with you before the world began."* (John 17:4-5)

B. Many of God's Significant Leaders had a Sense of Destiny Which Came from Their Life Purpose

Let me remind you of just a few of them:

1. Abraham (Gen. 12:1-3) knew that God would give him a land, make of him a great nation, and bring blessing to the earth through his descendants. *"Abram believed the LORD, and he credited it to him as righteousness."* (Gen. 15:6)

2. Moses was a hard sell (Exod. 1—4), but at the age of 80 he was captured by his call to lead the Israelites out of slavery.

3. Joshua knew he was called to lead the people across the Jordan and in the conquest of the Promised Land (Josh. 1). *"Now then, you and all these people, get ready to cross the Jordan River into the land I am about to give them—to the Israelites. I will give you every place where you set your foot, as I promised Moses."* (vv. 2-3)

4. John the Baptist lived with a driving sense of purpose. When questioned by priests and Levites, John confessed, *"I am not the Christ," "Are you the Prophet?" "No."*

"Who are you:?" "I am the voice." (John 1:20-23) He expressed his humility and gratitude when he said, *"He is the one who comes after me, the thongs of whose sandals I am not worthy to untie."* (John l :27) Later, following Jesus' conversation with Nicodemus, John the Baptist describes himself as Christ's friend and as the bridegroom's best man. His role was clear. *"The friend who attends the bridegroom waits and listens for him and is full of joy when he hears the bridegroom's voice. That joy is mine."* (John 3:29) Then, with great life focus, he says, "He must become greater; I must become less." (v. 30)

5. Paul's life purpose was first stated through the prophecy of a stranger named Ananias: *"This man is my chosen instrument to carry my name before the Gentiles and their kings and before the people of Israel."* (Acts 9:15) Paul's life purpose statement was simply profound:

"For to me, to live is Christ and to die is gain."
(Phil. 1:21)

Life is Christ—death is more of Christ. You can't lose; it's a win-win scenario.

Ask Christ for a clear sense of life purpose and hold on to this promise: *"And we know that in all things God works for the good of those who love him, who have been called according to his purpose. For those God foreknew he also predestined to be conformed to the likeness of his Son."* (Rom. 8:28-29)

C. Larry DeWitt's Life Purpose Statement

After pastoring my first church in Orangevale, California, for a few years, a request came for me to move back to the

Midwest and pastor a larger church in Flint, Michigan. I was very excited with what God was doing in California and had no desire for a change. I also had no idea how to go about making such a decision. I talked it through with a treasured friend who was a part of the church, Johnny Boswell, the leader of Sacramento Youth for Christ. He simply said, "I think you need to ask where you believe you will have the greater influence on people for Jesus Christ, if that's what your life is really about. That's how I've made such decisions." That life lesson became the basis of clarifying my life purpose:

Life Lesson **WHERE WILL I HAVE THE GREATEST INFLUENCE ON PEOPLE FOR JESUS CHRIST?**

After listening again to John the Baptist's words about his purpose, reflecting about God's grace and work in my life, and remembering Johnny Boswell's advice to me, I wrote a Life Purpose Statement. It hangs on the wall of my office and it is in the front of my Bible:

MY LIFE PURPOSE IS....

To influence as many people as possible, as much as possible, to be followers of Jesus Christ.

This is both a quantitative—how many?—and a qualitative—how much?—statement. I have challenged pastors, elders, and, for that matter, everyone in the congregation, to take time to reflect on their personal experiences, their perspective on how God uses them, their gifts and passions, and to write a specific Life Purpose Statement. Here are some samples:

- from Gordy Duncan, a pastor: "To love God with all my heart, soul, mind, and strength; to reflect Christ, and to point all people I encounter to Him."
- from Bob Feitl, a pastor: "To seek first God's kingdom, so I can significantly influence others in Christ."
- from Barney Hamady, a pastor: "To produce godly offspring."
- from Jim McCandliss, an elder who is a businessman: "To take on the character of the Lord Jesus and become a reflection of Him."
- from Paul Block, an elder who is a physician: "To bring glory to God through my relationships, by sharing the love of Jesus Christ with my family . . . with people I come in contact with, and by exercising my gifts of leadership, mercy, and encouragement."
- from Harry Frum, an elder who is a coach: "To serve people in Christ's name."

D. Clarify Your Life Purpose

On a typical California morning in June, it takes a while for the sun to burn off the fog. Sometimes our lives are like that.

Has the Son burned off the fog yet, so that you can clearly see the freeway he has put you on? If not, life will be tentative. You may keep asking, "Do I want to take the next exit . . . if I can even find it?" There is a lack of freedom in your spirit to move ahead with courage and get on with your life. There is added tension and apprehension. When the fog burns off, there is healthy perspective, a new sense of freedom, and new potential for clear vision about where you are headed.

Clear Life Purpose:

- Becomes a basis for our life planning
- Helps us sort out life's priorities
- Brings strength to our decision making
- Makes us more energetic servants of Christ
- Develops and encourages our passion for Christ and his Church

LET YOUR LIFE PURPOSE BECOME YOUR LIFE IMPERATIVE

E. Suggestions for Developing Your Life Purpose Statement

1. **Take some time in solitude.**

    a. Reflect back on your life perspective: (Chapters 1 & 2)

    "Who am I?"
    "Why am I here?"

    b. What thoughts from your Life and Times may be keys to understanding your life purpose?

    c. Review your Significant People and Essential Life Lessons project: What lessons may be the bases for your life purpose?

    d. Contemplate where and when and how God has used you most effectively.

    e. Reflect on your spiritual gifts

    f. Think about where and when you have found the greatest joy in your ministry.

2. **Discuss your Life Purpose with others** who are spiritually mature: your mate, your family, some trusted friends.
3. **Develop a one-or-two-sentence Statement of Life Purpose.** (It may take some refinement over a period of months.)
4. **Go public with it!** Share it with significant people in your life.

SECTION B.

THE PROMISE OF CHRIST

CENTERING IN CHRIST

"I will build my church" (Matt. 16:18)

3

PERSON, PROMISE, AND PRICE

Christ had been waiting for this day. He had carefully selected the site and prayerfully designed the event. He had taken his disciples north for a one-week retreat to Caesarea Philippi, which was located at the foot of Mt. Hermon, the dominating peak of Palestine, at 9,260 feet above sea level. The melting snows from Hermon form the sources of the Jordan River. One of these streams gushes from a huge cave in the rocky cliffs at Caesarea Philippi. It is a setting of rushing waterfalls, sparkling pools, serene meadows, majestic pines and flowering trees . . . one of the most beautiful and lush locations in all of Palestine.

Fourteen-hundred years before Christ, during the time of Joshua, the Canaanites came here to worship Baal, their god of fertility, and to offer child sacrifices. Four-hundred years before Christ, Pan, the Greek god of nature, was worshiped at the arches and altars, which remain and are being excavated even today. The city was even called Pan; it is from this god that we get our English word "panacea." The Arabic name for the site today is Panias or Banias. In 20 B.C., Herod the Great built a magnificent white marble temple to Caesar Augustus, both the emperor and the deity of the Roman world. Archaeologists have recently unearthed the foundations of this grand temple. It was enlarged and enhanced by his son, Herod Philip, who personalized the name of the city by adding his own name—Caesarea Philippi. Even today it is a place of worship for the Druze, a Muslim sect.

This was the precise setting Jesus chose for their retreat. Jesus was in his final year. The peak of his ministry was past; his ratings had dropped dramatically in the opinion polls. He had carefully calculated the questions and very clearly articulated them to his disciples. As they looked at the splendid temple to Caesar and the altars to the gods of previous cultures, he asked his disciples, *"Who do people say the Son of Man is?"* (Matt. 16:13)

Surveys say he was . . .

1. **John the Baptist,** Jesus' cousin, who came back to life. His ministry had been a sensation, but he had recently been beheaded by Herod Philip's brother, Herod Antipas.

2. **Elijah**, the prophet, who 900 years before was taken up to heaven in a whirlwind. He had led the face-off with the prophets of Baal on Mt. Carmel, and his return was prophesied in Malachi 4:5, the closing words of the Old Testament. *"See, I will send you the prophet Elijah before that great and dreadful day of the Lord comes."*

3. **Jeremiah**, the greatest of the Old Testament prophets.

A. Identify the Person – *"You are the Christ."* (Matt. 16:16)

Then Christ asked the crucial question, *"But what about you? Who do you say I am?"* (Matt. 16:15) And Peter, in an exceptional moment of clarity and wise judgment said, *"You are the Christ, the Son of the living God."* (v. 16) Jesus had waited for the day when the disciples would unequivocally identify him as unique from all the other gods the world recognized. The obvious implication for the disciples was to worship and revere only Jesus Christ in the place where many other gods had been recognized and revered. Jesus gave his blessing and emphasized that the revelation of himself was a gift from the Father in heaven.

I have spent some of my most memorable moments sitting at the foot of Mt. Hermon with fifty followers of Christ, simulating this Christ Retreat experience . . . looking at those altars that still exist . . . hearing the rush of the mighty waters from the peak of Mt. Hermon . . . asking again the crucial Christ question, "Who do you say I am?" . . . and hearing 20th-century disciples call out their answers in worship to the Lord. "You are my Savior." "You are my God." "You are my Best Friend." "You are my Hope." "You are my Good Shepherd." "You are my Rock." "You are my Living Water." "You are my Lord and Master," etc.

Imagine Jesus Christ looking you straight in the eyes today and asking, **"Who am I to you?"**

B. Claim Christ's Promise: *"I will build my church."* (Matt. 16:18)

- "'I"—Jesus set his future plans in motion.
- "'I will"—It was his will, not ours. The same God who, by the power of his word, willed this world into existence and created everything, now said, by that same will . . .

- "I will build"—The church is about building people, restoring broken people.
- "I will build my church"—It is his church, not ours.
- "and the gates of hell will not overcome it."— He meant he was about to face death and hell, but they could not destroy him. He meant that the Enemy would continue to work to break people down and distort God's truth, but he would not be able to impede the progress of Christ's church.

The calling of every Christian leader is to come to grips with who Jesus Christ is, and to be grabbed by this promise from him: "I will build my church."

What on earth is happening? Christ is building his Church! It may not be the headline when you pick up the Wall Street Journal, but it is the most significant thing happening on earth today.

C. Pay the Price — a Cross.

"Jesus began to explain to his disciples that he must go to Jerusalem." (Matt. 16:21) This time of retreat was a turning point in the Gospels. Jesus began to teach his disciples about the passion he felt regarding his coming Passion. It became a pressing divine imperative: he must go to Jerusalem and face the Cross.

Then he talked to them about their price: *"If anyone would come after me, he must deny himself and take up his cross and follow me."* (Matt. 16:24)

1. **Put Christ first:** self-denial . . . say NO to yourself; say YES to Jesus.

2. **Pay the price:** on a daily basis, you must get up and say, "I'll pay the price," whatever it takes, to put him first.
3. **Persistently follow:** keep walking with him, keep following him, keep obeying him. Some people are great starters—excited about faith in Christ—but they soon get tired of following.

The reason for this Caesarea Philippi spiritual retreat was that he had to know the disciples had come to grips with who he really was. Church leaders must come to grips with:

The Divine Person—Jesus is The Christ

The Divine Promise—He will build his Church

The Personal Cost—We must pay the price

All the planning and strategies we work so meticulously to develop will not accomplish the task, unless this life imperative is burning in our hearts with passion.

One week after the retreat came Christ's Transfiguration, when the select inner core of disciples saw his radiance and magnificence on the mountain, followed by his lesson about having a little bit of faith. *"I tell you the truth, if you have faith as small as a mustard seed . . . nothing will be impossible for you."* (Matt. 17:20-21)

These experiences signaled the beginning of the end for Christ. He set his face to go to Jerusalem, and he prayed that the disciples would set their faces to claim his promise for the church with a passion. He handed them the keys to the kingdom of heaven and encouraged them to unlock the gospel on earth. On the day of Pentecost, they did! As the Holy Spirit released the kingdom, 3,000 people believed in Christ, and the Church was off to a booming start.

I believe Christ's promise must be clear and must become the driving passion in the hearts of all pastors and church leaders; and with it, the confidence that what Christ intends to do, he will most certainly accomplish. I have become convinced that the primary reason I'm on earth is to participate in building Christ's Church.

Let Christ's promise become the focus of your passion.

4

PLACE OF PROMISE

How can we think about trusting God's promise without reference to Abraham's faith to believe the promise of God? *"By faith, Abraham, when called to go to a place he would later receive as an inheritance, obeyed and went, even though he did not know where he was going."* (Heb. 11:8)

A. Abraham's Promise – Call to the West Coast Promise, Promises

The promise God gave Abraham was quite straightforward: God would show him a place; God would raise up people; God would bless many people on earth. That would come through The Christ someday.

Pressures, pressures. There were pressures, lots of them: Abraham had to say farewell to his family of origin. (For some of you, that may not sound so bad!) He faced multiple moves; his move to the West Coast turned out to be four moves. He and his clan had to learn to survive on very little, because of famine in the new land. He encountered an unfamiliar culture and a different morality; faith in his marriage was tested by the stress of these cultural changes. Financial strain was certainly an issue, but God ultimately gave him prosperity.

A pastor must ask, "Do I feel called by God to be here, to be in this place?" That is more than a pastoral call from a group of people in a church. "Do I believe God is going to raise up a growing body of people for his name's sake?" "Do I envision God's blessing through the name, work, and glory of Christ?"

It will be quite easy for you to come up with a list as long—or longer—than Abraham's list of pressures, probably with some similarities. But go where God has called you with a sense of promise.

Life Lesson THERE ARE PRESSURES IN CLAIMING GOD'S PROMISES

God determines how those promises are to be fulfilled.

God determines the timing, as well. (Twenty-five years after the initial promise, Abraham and Sarah finally had a son.)

We, too, can be called to go, to a specific place, believing God will give us an inheritance. We must go, even though we don't know all that it entails.

B. Asking the Right Questions

My pastoral life had followed the typical pattern: three churches; serving three or four years in each pastorate. In four years, new sermons became more difficult, I got to really know the people, and probably more significantly, they got to know me. Each time I had moved, it was to a larger church, and I had taken one more step up the ecclesiastical ladder.

Within fifteen years I found myself in Fort Wayne, Indiana, pastoring the "Mother Church" of my denomination, The Missionary Church, across the street from our Bible college and the denominational headquarters. Now I had arrived. The question was, "but, where?" I kept asking myself one of my life questions . . . "Why me, Lord?" I wasn't sure of the why, but I was grateful for the opportunity.

When I first came to First Church, the mean age of the adult congregation was 55. God brought a whole new generation of people in their 30s and 40s into the church—300 or 400 of them. Most of the new believers were professional and business types. Hundreds of the Bible college students were attending, as well.

It didn't take a sophisticated study to discover that the people who were attending and coming to the Lord were, in fact, very different from the nucleus of the church I had come to pastor. There was elation that the church was growing, but there were increasing tensions caused by the cultural differences.

In a very important board meeting, an issue was addressed that caught me totally by surprise. Why had we changed the order of service? Since I had been pastor, we had been praying following the offering with thanks, rather than anticipating the offering with the prayer that people would give. I wasn't even aware of my insensitivity in changing this tradition.

At another board meeting, the newest member (and a fairly new believer) said, "Why don't we just divide the church . . . we really do have two churches!" The room became silent, because he had accurately analyzed the situation. There were, in fact, two different congregations, and they weren't mixing very well. The newer nucleus was really a threat to the old guard. In that process God was helping me discover the people he had designed me to be most effective with.

I found myself busy four nights a week with boards and committee meetings, more controlled by others' expectations and less controlled by my own heart. I got caught up with handling the less significant and chasing trivial pursuits.

Things were going well. There was no significant pressure for me to leave. There were tensions, and the steps of progress that I felt had to come, came painfully and with a great deal of pressure. Without even being aware of it, my energy and motivation were being drained. The many demands of a larger pastoral responsibility increased my burden. Rather than doing more of the King's business, I was consumed with the "busyness" of running the business of the church.

There was a growing dissatisfaction in my heart that I couldn't even admit to myself. I began to ask significant questions . . . questions which I believe all pastors ask:

Who am I most effective in influencing for Christ?

Where do I fit?

Howard Hendricks, Dallas Seminary professor, came to town to teach a citywide marriage and family conference I had organized. As I drove him to lunch, we had a conversation that impacted the direction of my life and ministry. "DeWitt, is it really happening at old First Church?" I hesitated and finally replied that some good things were happening and the church was growing. Then he said, in his penetrating manner, "If it's going to happen, get to it. If not, get where it can, as soon as you can. You've only got one life; make it count!" That five-minute conversation set the stage in my mind for the transition and call that were to follow.

Am I really doing what God wants me to do with my life?

What percentage of my time do I spend doing what the church "system" asks of me?

What percentage of what I am doing is to satisfy the expectations of others?

What percentage of what I am doing is what I believe God has called me to do as a pastor?

Is this larger responsibility more freeing or more limiting?

I was trying too hard to do what I thought was expected of me; it was time for me to commit to being more concerned about doing what God wanted me to do. God was teaching me one of life's most significant lessons:

Life Lesson FEAR GOD MORE THAN YOU FEAR PEOPLE

It was a Saturday afternoon in Fort Wayne. A phone call came from out of the blue: well, actually, from the Twin Peaks Conference Center in the San Bernardino Mountains of Southern California. It was one of those phone calls we all get from time to time . . .

I was asking myself, "How do I get rid of this call politely and quickly?" The conversation and approach were quite direct. Dr. Larry Parks, a lay leader of a small Missionary Church in Thousand Oaks, California, had the audacity to ask if I would be open to resigning at First Church and coming to California to be their new pastor. Trying to be courteous, I said, "Well, tell me something about your church. He straightforwardly shared that the church had grown from 120 to 60 in the past three years. But three couples at this church were going to do something fresh and significant. They were inviting me to consider becoming their new pastor and a missionary to Southern California. I then talked briefly with John Wimber, who shared with me that Thousand Oaks was a growing, exciting, and needy community; and that these people were eager for God to do something fresh in reaching that community.

There are many older, smaller churches in America that are terminally ill. Some slip into a coma and die quietly . . . others die desperately. Some, in their state of hopelessness, are ready for resuscitation and a new start. These people had a sense of holy desperation that made them willing to try something new and innovative. I was not as aware of this desperation as they were, but my heart was inwardly desperate for a fresh start, as well.

C. My Call to the West Coast

With a polite "Thanks," I let go of that conversation and hung up the receiver; but my heart was still on the line. Although I tried several times, I could not bring myself to call back and say, "No, thanks." So, within a couple of weeks, Beccy and I decided to make a whirlwind trip to Thousand Oaks. We discovered a terminally ill church, ready for a new start. Since I had begun my D. MIN. in Church Growth at Fuller Seminary, I saw myself as a potential consultant to help them sort out issues and answer the question, "What would it actually take for God to give us a new beginning?" Saturday, we had a board meeting and discussed many of the issues raised in answer to that question.

The leaders had been studying church growth materials and were really ready for something new from the Lord. Out of that meeting came a list of fifteen key concepts succinctly summarized.

At least, the list gave us a start in answering the question, "What would it take to see this old church become a new church . . . the new Calvary Community Church of the Conejo Valley?"

Sunday morning, I spoke to a booming crowd of 50 people, yet somehow I seemed to feel more inspired than when speaking to 1,000 the Sunday before.

Monday morning, while shaving (that's always a time when my mind is stimulated and lots of significant thoughts surface)—how about you? That day, I walked into the bedroom with a stunned look and a half-shaven face, and I said to Beccy, "In two days, people here have shown more willingness to risk change to see the church really happen than the people in the church we are now serving have been willing to risk in three years."

D. Match Points

1. **People match:** We did the typical things: we went to the Chamber of Commerce and gathered information about the community; we drove the area; we checked out the churches; we checked out the schools; we even shocked ourselves by putting down a $500 deposit on a house to be built sometime the following year. As I examined the community, I realized that the people who lived there were very similar to the people I had been effective in reaching in Indiana.

2. **Passion match:** We drove around Westlake Village, a city of 15,000 people without one evangelical church, and we wept. Here was a beautiful, master-planned community;

yet no church was communicating The Master's Plan with biblical authority! As I tried to get a grip on the Conejo Valley, God put a grip on my heart. I began to feel the same driving passions for this community that these few families who formed the nucleus of the church had developed.

3. **Price match:** A month after I returned home, and just before I walked into a church board meeting, I received a phone call from Dr. Larry Parks. He said, "I just want you to know that the key families of the church are ready to go. We'll take out second mortgages on our houses to provide the funds to see this new church happen, if that becomes necessary." It was the confirmation that the people at Calvary were willing to pay the price, and they were asking us to join them in that spirit of sacrifice. That night, I walked away from the phone call, walked into the board meeting and informed the members that I was resigning to join some courageous Southern Californians in the resuscitation of a dying Missionary Church. Paying the price for us meant:

    1. letting go of my role as senior pastor of a historic, prestigious church
    2. a willingness to start all over again at nearly 40 years old
    3. accepting half the salary we'd been accustomed to receiving; that is, if the Lord provided
    4. taking our children out of a wonderful private Christian school environment and enrolling them in a public California school

    We soon discovered how much we were owned by the system. We drove a new Buick LaSabre, leased by the church. We lived in a lovely home in a fine residential area—the church parsonage. As we released the keys to a car and a home, it released our hold on our sense of security, the very environment in which we'd lived. We excitedly accepted the challenges of our great adventure.

4. **Peace match:** When I announced my resignation to the church, people expressed loving thanks to us. God had done wonderful things and changed many of their lives, and the people had been very good to us. But I discovered that God gives a heart release when he gives a new call. I think it was important that we didn't have to leave; but we felt called to leave; we didn't leave in defeat. We told people we had been called to be missionaries to pagan Southern California. The percentage of unchurched people in California was greater than in some areas of the world where the church was supporting missionaries. Being a Missionary Church, that sat well with the people. With the impressions people had of Southern California, a church that had sent missionaries to other places in the world certainly needed to send some there! They just didn't expect it to be their pastor.

People talked to my wife more than they did to me about why we were leaving. When asked if it was hard to let go of the security of what we had, Beccy—this courageous, fearless lady—could honestly say no. People asked about the size of the church. When she told them they had 40 or 50 members, they didn't know how to respond except to ask, "Well, what kind of salary have they offered you?" Her answer . . . "Hopefully half of what we are receiving now."

Larry DeWitt was certainly going out on a very slim limb . . . maybe he was having a midlife crisis!

There were questions we expected to be asked, like, *Will we really survive in the Southern California culture? What if this new church doesn't happen? What if the financial support isn't there?* We were letting go of lots of security. We were believing that it was really going to happen. We were going for broke, and there was no turning back. But God gave us an incredible sense of peace about it all. We were not frivolous about it, but we were care-less. *"Do not be anxious about anything, but in everything, by prayer and petition, with thanksgiving, present your requests to God. And the peace of God, which transcends all understanding, will guard your hearts and your minds in Christ Jesus."* (Phil 4:6-7) We had prayed about it and had been specific in our requests, that God would provide clarity about the call, would direct in seeing this new church happen, and would provide the support necessary. He did give us peace that transcended the human rational factors. Our minds were not troubled. Our hearts were calm. The signs of God's hand and provision were already evident.

We sent out a letter to a nucleus of friends from the past who had believed in my ministry, to relatives, and even to a few from First Church, explaining the mission and asking for their financial support. We told them we needed help with salary, the move to a new location, and advertising to see this new church happen. We had even chosen a few individuals we thought could make significant larger contributions to our support. Would you believe that the day I resigned, one of those couples asked us over for lunch. I remember sitting there trying to get up my courage to ask if they would be willing to make a significant contribution. I caught my breath and paused ten more seconds before asking. That was the ten seconds God wanted. They then volunteered that when I had resigned and described our new ministry that morning, God had put on their hearts—separately, though simultaneously—to commit $5,000 to help us get started. There were a few other experiences like that, affirming God's calling and provision.

5. **Purpose match:** The Life Purpose Statement that had become the driving passion of my life several years before helped me to make this critical decision.

MY LIFE PURPOSE IS … To influence as many people as possible, as much as possible, to be followers of Jesus Christ.

We believed in our hearts that within five years we would have a greater influence on a greater number of people than if we had stayed with the program in Fort Wayne. In fact, it happened.

The day finally came in the last week in January when we were to say farewell. It's not easy to say goodbye, and it has never been easy for us to say goodbye to a congregation. I think that's the way it should be. They had planned an evening farewell reception and send-off for us. That afternoon, an Indiana ice storm hit the city. It was almost impossible to go out. We made it the two blocks to the church for that going-away reception and were greeted by only a handful of the congregation. The next morning, five of us and our Samoyed dog piled into our "previously owned" Mercury, recently purchased for $600, towing our 26-foot temporary hometrailer. Our neighbors literally pushed the car and trailer out of the driveway, up the street and around the comer to a major road. With a chilling, icy departure, and with our hearts full of hope, we began to slide southwest. Several days later, as we drove into Thousand Oaks, California, we knew that God had not called us to our next three-year pastorate, but he had prepared us to lay down our lives for the flock he would raise up in the Conejo Valley.

6. **Promise match:** With our first view of the valley, I had a deep sense of promise that Christ, in fact, would build his church here, and we would be privileged to be a part of it. Rather than "seeing is believing"—in faith,—"believing is seeing."

   "Now faith is being sure of what we hope for and certain of what we do not see." (Heb. 11:1) There was no church to see yet, but we saw it in our hearts and felt certain it would happen.

Let Christ put you in your place!

5

THE PREMISE OF CALVARY COMMUNITY—FAITH IS FUN!

"Faith is fun"—most of the time! *"Without faith it is impossible to please God,"* (Heb. 11:6) It doesn't say it is improbable—"it is impossible . . . because anyone who comes to him must believe that he exists and that he rewards those who earnestly seek him." (6b)

Faith is part of pleasing God, and pleasing God is where the fun in life comes from!

A. Clear Assumptions

When we met with the board on our first visit to Thousand Oaks, they voted to adopt the 15 principles they had decided on the day before, and to extend a pastoral call to me, to give five years to implementing those principles. On Sunday, November 2, 1975, a nucleus of 21 members of the Calvary Community voted unanimously to implement the following:

- **BIBLICAL OBJECTIVES:** (1) That the Biblical Objectives of the church be clarified and established in writing.
- **OUR COMMITMENT:** (2) That the pastor and board recognize Jesus Christ as the Head of this church and commit themselves to the Biblical Objectives as the basis for future planning and decision making.
- **ORGANIZATION:** (3) That a new church organization and by-laws be developed, based on the Biblical Objectives.
- **TIME INVESTMENT:** (4) That each board member plan to invest a minimum of one-half day per week in the work of the church, in addition to church services.
- **PLANNING:** (5) That the leaders meet for quarterly planning days, for the purpose of planning the future.
- **TRAINING & DISCIPLING:** (6) That training people for ministry and discipling others have a place of priority in church planning.
- **MEMBERSHIP:** (7) That church membership be based on personal faith in Jesus Christ and public identification with him and the church through water baptism.
- **LEADERSHIP:** (8) That the biblical standards of leadership be taught and become the basis of church leadership and elections.
- **LOCATION CHANGE:** (9) That we plan toward a change in church location, to better identify with the community and the people we are to reach.

- **ZERO BUDGETING:** (10) That priority items be determined and budgeted as the first step in planning the church budget.
- **STAFF:** (11) That secretarial help be secured initially, and that the pastoral staff be enlarged within a year, if possible.
- **CONSULTANTS:** (12) That John Wimber, of Fuller Evangelistic Association, and Gordon Mollett, of the Western District of the Missionary Church, be consulted in planning strategy and church organization.
- **SERVICE SCHEDULE:** (13) That the schedule of regular services be changed, based on our church objectives and to free people for ministries.
- **SCRIPTURE:** (14) That we use the versions of Scripture which we believe best communicate God's Word to men and women.
- **PASTORAL CALLING:** (15) That the pastor be given a 5-year call.

These 15 theses were put in writing . . . if they had not been written permanently in the record, times would have come when emotionally we would have backed away from these commitments.

B. First-Year Goals

We arrived in the Conejo Valley and parked our trailer and car in the side yard of Dr. Larry and Sally Parks' home. They had graciously offered to let us to live beside them until we had a home. They had no idea that the projected three weeks would extend to three months. We had also agreed to hold services in the old church building for a few weeks, until a new location could be identified. I would like to tell you that the church immediately exploded. Not so. I soon learned that it takes far more energy to get off the launch pad than it does to stay in orbit. It takes far more energy and time to prepare for the resuscitation of a dying church than I had anticipated.

Purpose, purpose, purpose

It is an effort in futility to try to bring about change in the existing church, unless people are first grabbed with the passion about what Christ wants to do. We spent extensive time together in weekly Bible studies and prayer meetings, talking about what Christ wanted to accomplish. "How will we get our church to grow?" "How will we get people to come?"

These were not the primary questions, not even the right questions. "What does Christ want to see happen?" "How can we cooperate with his purpose?" These were the valid questions, and still are.

Answers to these questions must be discovered by people and pastor together.

I joined laypeople who were developing a passion to see Christ's Purpose happen. I've often watched pastors go to a conference and leave ready to change the world (at least their world). They go home and start doing it . . . without the participation of people in the body. It is imperative that people in the body and the pastor together develop a passion to see a new day come. People must be part of the process if they are to catch the dream with you.

Prayer and passion

I was captured by the courage and commitment of the handful of people who had made that initial phone call to me in Indiana. We began having small group prayer gatherings, asking such questions as, "What do you think Christ would really like to do in this valley?" That is where all the church growth theory moved from head to heart. That's where, timidly, yet courageously, people like Marsha said, "I believe Christ would like to bring 1,000 people to himself and to this church in the next 5 years. Is that ridiculous to pray?" Then, she prayed it.

Those prayer gatherings were so critical, because—the calling to see the Church of Christ happen had to become a driving mandate in the hearts of the leadership.

We began to pray for little things, too, and then watch them come about. We'd say, wouldn't it be marvelous if such-and-such could happen...?—but that would take a miracle! We'd pray about it, and one by one, big and little miracles took place. We knew that the things that were happening could not have been engineered by people . . . God was doing it!

Cultural and community analysis

Where do you start? Literally, the first week we were in Thousand Oaks, we went out to dinner with Dr. Larry and Sally Parks and Bill and Cheryl Haas. Bill was the executive director of the Chamber of Commerce for Thousand Oaks, and he was doing his thing by having dinner with a new pastor in town. For three hours that evening we pumped him with questions about the kinds of people who lived in the community, their needs, what needs were being met well, and what needs were not being addressed yet. We discussed the kinds of pressures people lived with, being a bedroom community for Los Angeles. We asked what the greatest concerns were of the community leaders. Bill Haas went home somewhat stunned by our conversation. He couldn't understand why church leaders were so interested in the people of the community.

I immediately began a two-week course in Church Growth Principles and Procedures with Dr. Peter Wagner at Fuller Theological Seminary. God's timing is perfect. The specific assignment for the course was to write a five-year analysis and strategy for planting a new church. For me it was hardly theory; it was the fact of life.

We quickly began as thorough a demographic study as anyone had done of the Conejo Valley: Who lived here, and what were the residential growth patterns? There was a far higher level of people with college educations/graduation than the population norms, even for California. The population bubbles were pre and early teens, and people in their late 30s and early 40s. Professional and technically skilled people composed the largest segment of the population; followed by managerial/administrative roles. Of the total work force of the Conejo Valley, 56 percent fell into those categories, with only 1 to 2 percent laborers. Daily, 60 percent commuted to the greater Los Angeles area.

We did a careful study of the few people who were presently in the Calvary Community Church. The church had peaked at 95 members, with a record high attendance of 115 eight years before. We saw that the profile of the people in the church was strikingly different than the community they were praying to reach—rather than being primarily professional, comprised of technically skilled people in their 30s and 40s, thirteen members were senior citizens who lived in a trailer park across the street from the church; sixty-five percent of the congregation's wage earners were semiskilled laborers; and the church was located in "Old Town," where few of the people moving to the valley would ever drive

The existing leadership recognized this profile disparity and knew that the church must go through a dramatic shift to accomplish its mission.

Initial one-year goal

First-year goal: believe God for 15 committed families, representative of the community. They would be sought through transfer growth; perhaps mature Christians moving into the area and still attending church in Los Angeles or the San Fernando Valley.

Faith is fun! On the last Sunday of that first year, two families came up to me and said, "We want to join this church as a part of our New Year's commitment." When that second family told me that, I shouted, "Praise God; you're an answer to prayer and God's goal for this church!" They had no idea what I was so excited about; but they were literally the 14th and 15th families to make a commitment to the new Calvary Community that first year.

I couldn't wait to come back the first Sunday of the New Year and tell the congregation. We had prayed in faith for 15 families committed by the end of the year, and God had given us precisely 15 on the last Sunday of the year.

It was as though those 15 specific principles the congregation had voted on before I came as their pastor became the "theses" nailed on the door. We began implementing those principles, such as:

- **Biblical Objectives:**

The single most important factor in launching the new church was to write a Statement of Biblical Purpose, or Biblical Objectives. We met together on Sunday evenings to clarify and establish in writing the distinctive purposes of the church. Why are we here? That is the most important question. The church board established a task force of five people to give direction in establishing those Biblical Objectives.

"that the Biblical Objectives of the church be clarified and established in writing."

Once we had completed those Sunday night studies, we had a comprehensive written Statement of Biblical Purpose that would become the driving force for almost everything; i.e., choosing leaders, establishing membership, overall planning, deciding programs and schedules.

- **Membership:**

"that the Church membership be based on personal faith in Jesus Christ and public identification with Him in the church through water baptism."

I remember a very critical turning point in a board meeting at the First Church in Ft. Wayne prior to coming to Thousand Oaks. In discussing membership applications, one young man, obviously converted and alive in Christ, went home for Christmas every year. His father made Christmas wine for the family; it was a lifelong tradition. Yet with the pure conscience and intentions of a young Christian, he asked, "How can I go home and participate with my family in drinking Christmas wine, if a commitment to not drink any alcoholic beverages is part of the commitment to be a member of this church?" He sought my counsel. His conclusion was to go home and enjoy that Christmas celebration with his father and not offend him by rejecting the Christmas wine. Yet the board was struggling with " . . . can we accept this person into membership? He doesn't meet our requirements."

In another situation, a blind woman had seen the light of who Jesus Christ is and was marvelously converted. She belonged to a society of which we as a church did not approve, and her medical and life insurance were through this organization. Her response to us was, "Do you want me to drop my membership in the organization? If that's what it takes to be part of the church, I'll be glad to. What do you suggest I do about my insurance?" We struggled as a board with the issue of her membership, yet we were not ready to assume responsibility for her insurance needs. Something suddenly dawned on me, and I shared my sentiments with the board, I think to their chagrin: "It seems to me that it is much more difficult to get into this church than it is to get into heaven. Something about that just doesn't make sense."

These and other experiences led to this conviction that church membership at Calvary would be based on personal faith in Jesus Christ and public identification with him and the church through water baptism. Romans 15:7 became a very significant verse to me regarding church membership. "Accept one another, then, just as Christ accepted you, in order to bring praise to God." Calvary would be a church that accepted people on the basis of their personal faith in Christ . . . as a part of his family . . . no strings attached. We literally dissolved the existing church membership and started all over again.

- **Leadership:**

  "that the biblical standards of leadership be taught and become the basis of church leadership and elections."

The existing church board voted to establish themselves as an interim board, until a new church leadership structure was put in place. I remember asking the critical question, "Suppose God brings other people to this church within a year who fit the qualifications of leadership more than you do? Would you be willing to relinquish that role to them?" That was a tough issue to deal with emotionally, yet they courageously went on record saying, "Yes!" Within six months we established a Bible study group with potential new leaders and studied Gene Getz's, *The Measure of a Man*. As we studied these qualifications for elders, different people in the group led the discussion each week. After 12 weeks or so, the day finally came. We asked everyone present to write the names of those in the group they felt comfortable suggesting as elders for Calvary Community. Would you believe that everyone in the group wrote down the same four people? The Holy Spirit gave clear direction about the founding eldership for Calvary Community. This exciting evidence of the Holy Spirit's leading was immediately shared with the congregation. "Faith is fun!"

- **Location change:**

  "that we plan toward a change in church location, to better identify with the community and the people we are to reach."

We indeed planned toward a change of church location, to better identify with the community and the people we were there to reach. Folks had prayed for years for people to come to their church in this economically depressed part of town, but they didn't come. We needed new cultural eyes. I remember the first time I walked into the building. I looked up at the ceiling. It had been designed for ceiling tiles. The former pastor proudly shared with me that someone had donated some Styrofoam squares that were the same size. They were able to use those instead of buying ceiling tiles. What he saw as a sign of God's provision, I saw as a barrier to the people who lived in the community who had an eye for excellence.

We asked the question, ***"Where's the most visible meeting place in town?"*** The answer came quickly: The Los Robles Country Club is the "happening place"; the Chamber of Commerce dinners and other civic events happened there. Where was it located? We discovered it was visible from the freeway corridor, accessible, and centrally located. But they'd never agree to let us meet there! Within five weeks we were, in fact, scheduled to meet and have our first Sunday Service—"Celebration"—in this new location. I received a call from the director of the Chamber, Bill Haas, on Thursday saying, "You'd better come to my office immediately. I have some troubling news to share with you." He told me that the restaurant operators had fallen behind in their financial obligations, that marshals would come in, chain the doors and shut down the business the next day. This would make scandalous headlines in the newspaper the very week we were to begin services there. Bill's quick P.S. was, "Don't worry, I've already arranged things. If you want to go ahead and have your church start there Sunday, the doors will be unlocked and the heat will be turned on."

It was all set . . . and we did! On April 5, 1976, the Calvary Community started in its new location. God had an amusing way of giving free advertising to this new church, on the front page of the newspaper! And this director of the Chamber of Commerce, an avowed anti-church guy, showed up for our first

Celebration. Two months later, on Easter Sunday, he was one of the first to make a commitment to Christ. Along with him, a father of a church family, Bill Gregory, for whom the people of the church had prayed for 20 years, made his commitment to Christ also. This sparked the timber and brought fire to our faith!

Children's Celebration center: But where will the children meet? Where was the finest, most well-equipped children's facility in town? The answer—The Young Set Club—but they'd never allow us to use it. I went there and talked with Marv Schmidt, the director. After our conversation, he said, "I am an atheistic Jew, but when I hear what you want to do to help make families healthy and meet their needs, I feel like we have a lot in common. Several churches have asked to meet here before, but I've never given it a serious thought. I'm amazed at myself, but—you are welcome to meet here if you wish!" That location became our new children's Sunday morning celebration center.

- **Service Schedules:**

  "that the schedule of regular services be changed, based on our church objectives and to free people for ministries."

When will we meet? What will we do? Those decisions were made based on the Biblical Objectives and with the desire to free people's busy schedules so that they could minister. I remember someone asking, "Aren't we going to have Sunday night services? Somewhere?" I asked the leaders, "Well, what Biblical Objectives will be met by having a Sunday evening service, that are not going to be met in some other way?" And, "Why do you really come to Sunday evening services?" Somewhat reluctantly, each of them admitted that they came to church on Sunday night because they were used to it, felt guilty if they didn't attend, and felt they ought to be there because they were leaders. Sorry, but we needed better reasons than that for having a Sunday night service.

- **Scripture:**

  "that we use the versions of Scripture which we believe best communicate God's Word to men and women."

  What version of the Bible will we use? We had previously committed to choose a version that would communicate God's Word effectively to the people we were trying to reach. We decided to use only the New International Version (NIV) for adults, teens, and children.

THE ISSUE IS NOT THE ISSUE . . . You see, in each of these above-described situations, the issue was not the issue. The real issue was: how will we make the appropriate decisions, based on the Biblical Purpose we've established, and based on the people we are trying to reach?

Staying the course:

Thank God for that original document, the Statement of Purpose, and the commitment to take bold and courageous steps to rebirth this church. Within a few weeks, a special board meeting was held as the tensions increased. I realized that there is an emotional time lag that takes place in the process of change. People had voted to make changes, yet somehow these decisions left a knot in the pits of their stomachs. A sincere couple, very committed to Christ, came one week to this country club banquet room with a bar in the comer where we were now meeting, and they went home traumatized. When I met with them they said, "Sorry pastor, we know we voted to do this, but somehow it just doesn't seem right to us to be meeting in that country club, when this church we worked so hard to build is sitting empty on Sunday mornings. We just can't come back."

This forced a very critical and courageous decision: We

must stay the course. A few of us sat down and discussed the implications for this couple and others who felt the same. If we backed away from this dream, this vision of seeing a new church happen, because the decisions were traumatic for some of the members, what would be the result? The people whom Christ had placed us here to reach would probably never be reached. The mission would not be accomplished. But if we stayed the course, what about these few people who were being bruised in the process? They wouldn't be lost to the Kingdom. There were other traditional, conservative churches in town where they could go. I cried and prayed with those people, because I felt the honest hurt and struggle they were having. They had voted for the decisions to change, but emotionally they just found it to be too much.

In Hebrews 12:1-2, we read, "Let us throw off everything that hinders and the sin that so easily entangles, and let us run with perseverance the race marked out for us. Let us fix our eyes on Jesus, the author and perfecter of our faith."

The tough decision was to fix our eyes on Jesus and the people who needed him, realizing that we would create tension and pressure for some people in the church. Some new families came, but the church wasn't growing, because others began to leave. I wish I could say the transition was all easy, but it wasn't. The emotional implications of change are very demanding.

The Parks and DeWitts met on a Sunday night. The question was, which one of the original families was going to leave next? God gave us an important insight:

Life Lesson **DEAL WITH THE DIFFICULTIES, BUT DON'T DOUBT THE DREAM**

"God's gifts and his call are irrevocable." (Rom. 11:29) We said to one another, "We're committed to seeing this church happen, even if every other founding family leaves. But let's be honest in dealing with the difficulties." We quickly identified primary concerns:

1. **We needed good, contemporary music**
2. **Something had to happen—for teens and young adults.**
3. **These became immediate matters of open prayer.** Within two weeks, God answered. I met Ken Waggoner, from Continental Ministries, and we had an instant Sunday morning Continentals Chorale. The next week, Ken Schaub, new to the church, came up and said, "My heart is with high school- and college-age young people. Is there a way I can help meet with those people and get something going?" God answered specific prayers with specific answers.

Share: Share the needs and, equally important, share faith reports of God's answers. We made it part of the pattern of the first year to share specific concerns, and to give faith reports back to the congregation. We celebrated and rejoiced over specific victories.

Model: We believed that God had called us to be a model church for others in the '80s.

"You became imitators of us and of the Lord; in spite of severe suffering, you welcomed the message with the joy given you by the Holy Spirit. And so, you became a model to all the believers in Macedonia and Achaia. The Lord's message rang out from you not only in Macedonia and Achaia—your faith in God has become known everywhere." (1 Thess. 1:6-8)

We were off the launch pad . . . it really began to happen. People began to come. Many met Christ. In September 1979, we had to start dual Celebrations to accommodate the rapid growth. The manager of the restaurant and banquet facility where we were meeting came to me one Sunday and said, "Reverend, we have a problem." I thought it had been a great morning; I hadn't seen any problems. He continued, "Do you know how many people we had at brunch today in the restaurant? Just a few tables. Do you know why? Because the parking lot was filled with cars for your church. Now, Reverend, I have nothing against your church, but why don't you find a new place to meet? No hurry . . . sometime in the next 30 days!"

God pushed us out of that building to look for a new location. Clay Nicholson, a wonderful, retired gentleman in the congregation, went on a search to find a new home for Calvary. Could it be a movie theater, a school, a community building, an empty building in a shopping mall? What about a warehouse? The only available facility we found was a new warehouse in an industrial park nearing completion.

Together we chose a theme . . . "GO FOR IT!" We had a gentleman in the church, Brad Greene, who wrote themes for Argus posters. He submitted the "Go For It" motto and, would you believe, it became a national by-line. The birth of the warehouse church for Calvary Community was part of popularizing the words "Go For It" in the American culture.

As we made the bold decision to move into this new location, the same old emotional pressure was there that we had faced when we moved from our little "A-frame" church to the country club. The warehouse was four times as big as the restaurant where we had been meeting. There were doubters who said, "It's way too big; it's too impersonal." There were the spirit-dampeners who like to throw cold water on things, who said, "See the financial pressures this has created? If God really wanted us here, he would provide the finances, wouldn't he?" The move was time-intensive, and we had to work through the tensions.

On March 23, 1980, it happened! Celebration took place at our new warehouse . . . one week before the fourth anniversary of the rebirth of Calvary Community Church.

One year after moving into the warehouse, we celebrated our fifth anniversary. Somehow, I convinced Dr. Peter Wagner to come and speak. During the service, he caught me by surprise by asking, "By the way, how many members do you have now? Your goal when you launched the church was to have 500 members by your fifth anniversary." I had not been thinking specifically about that. The secretary, sitting near the front of the church, answered, "We have 497 members now, and our average attendance has just reached 1,000." In a flash of inspiration, I turned to the congregation and said, "Are there any people present who want to join the church today?" Five people raised their hands. We literally surpassed our five-year goal for membership on the very day we celebrated our fifth anniversary! **Faith is Fun!**

By the end of that year, even dual Celebrations were inadequate. Soon the warehouse was too crowded. A balcony was added, and later we added another Sunday morning service.

We conducted a survey, asking people in the body what other time might be an acceptable time to come to church. Saturday evening seemed to be the most acceptable time, so we began to announce, "Saturday Night Alive at Six."

Bill Hybels cautioned me to not just begin Saturday night services, but to prepare by asking people to own the vision with me. We asked for 400 people to make a four-month commitment to attend and 40 workers to service children's ministries, ushering, etc. After a month of response, we had close to 400 people committed to being a part of launching the new Saturday Night Celebration. I remember that first Saturday evening; I admit I had some anxiety, wondering what would actually happen. Would those 400 people show up? How many people would flake? Would others come to check it out?

I walked into the room . . . 800 people were there. I trembled and wept . . . and I knew that Saturday Night Celebrations were going to happen.

Set goals . . . share them with people . . . and expect them to happen, not for the sake of numerical accomplishment, but for the sake of faith. **Faith is fun!!**

Accomplishing goals you've reached for motivates other people to believe God for what they know he wants to do in their lives.

Christ keeps fulfilling his promise, "'I will build my church." The most important venture happening on earth is this: **Jesus Christ is building his Church.**

LET CHRIST'S PROMISE BECOME YOUR DRIVING MINISTRY MANDATE.

Pastoral leadership is like a game I am sure you have all played—a game of nerves. Have you taken a rubber band and asked someone to hold the other end? You start pulling just a little. At first you laugh, but as you begin to put more tension on the band, the stress advances exponentially for both of you, and it becomes a test of nerves. If you pull too hard, the rubber band snaps, and you both get stung.

Pastors need to know how to apply the right amount of tension on the rubber band to encourage people to move from their comfort zone; but not too much that it creates extensive anxiety and sets up resistance. Very little pull means that the congregation isn't being challenged to grow. Pull too hard or too fast, and everyone gets stung; the rebirth of the church aborts, and pastors leave, sadly disappointed, disillusioned and embittered toward people, and sometimes even toward the Lord.

SECTION C.
PRIORITIES OF THE CHURCH

PRIORITIES IN ORDER

We've all heard it. We've all said it. Practically every pastor on earth has counseled it. *"You need to get your priorities straightened out."* You had better decide what is most important to you in life. First things first. Get your life in order. There are some priorities that must be in place for you to do well in life. Without priorities, your life will lack direction.

We must say the same thing about the church:

- Get your church's priorities straightened out
- Decide what is important to the life of the church
- First things first in the church
- Get your church life in order
- Priorities must be in place for the church to do well
- Without priorities the church will lack direction

A. Six Basic Assumptions About Priorities

Priorities are essential. They are as essential for the life of the church as they are for our personal lives. People get in trouble when their priorities are not in the right order and when they are not clear.

Priorities are sequential. Churches will be in trouble if their priorities are not in the right order, and there *is* a right order; there *is* an effective order. Improper sequence will bring inadequate results.

Priorities are inferential. There are subtle and not-so-subtle pervasive implications which penetrate the entire church culture. They reflect what is really important and what is not so important to us.

Priorities are referential. They become our points of reference, the basis for tough decision making, and the primary grid against which we measure ourselves.

Priorities are influential. They influence everything about the church and the way we do church.

Priorities are consequential. There are serious consequences for not having clear priorities: families are destroyed, marriages erupt, businesses fail, and people miss their potential for accomplishments and healthy relationships. One of the most glorious passages about the church in the New Testament is found in Ephesians 3. *"Now to him who is able to do immeasurably more than all we ask or imagine . . . to him be glory in the church."* (v. 20) It is possible to miss God's immeasurably more. It is possible to "do" church without Christ receiving the glory he deserves. This can be the natural consequence of wrong priorities.

One of my greatest concerns about Christ and eternity is discovering the immeasurably more that he would like to have done in and through my life and in the church where I serve . . . how much more he would have and could have done.

Four Primary Priorities:

I developed Four Priorities (**Ps**), and they have proved to be very helpful, not only for church growth analyses; they have also been effectively used by Christian businessmen in establishing clear priorities in their businesses.

Priority #1 – PURPOSE

Purpose is ***why*** we exist. Before an archer draws a bow, he identifies his target. If the target isn't clear, he won't hit it.

Before one ventures into a new business, he had better decide what he is trying to accomplish. In the church, it is somewhat different. The question is not, "What would *we* like to accomplish?" but "What would *he* like to accomplish?" The single most important question the church can ever ask is, "What would Jesus Christ, the Head of the Church, like to accomplish?" The target needs to be clear and specific.

When I have asked pastors, *"What is the Purpose of the Church?"* the most frequent answer is to quote the Great Commission, Matthew 28:19-20. Right on! Going—making disciples of all nations—baptizing them—teaching them. And then, Christ gave the closing assurance that he would be with them in the effort, till the completion of the age. Christ, and his Purpose for his church, must be our primary priority. Can we expand on it?

Key Question: Why does Christ's Church exist on earth?

We will focus on this question in Chapter 7.

Priority #2 – PEOPLE

People are ***who*** we are. Who are the people in the church? Who are the people in the community we feel called to reach? Do we know them and understand them? Do the people in the church know and understand that Christ and his Purpose is Number 1, and they are Number 2 on the priority list? When you are Number 2, you always struggle to be Number 1. In essence, the Christian life is about recognizing Jesus Christ as Number 1 and struggling to keep ourselves in our place . . . Number 2.

Key Question: Who are the people we are uniquely called to serve and reach?

Priority #3 – PROGRAM

Program is ***how*** we do it. Christ and his scriptural Purpose are sacred. Programs are not. Too often, pastors in churches focus on Program. They attend seminars and conferences looking for the right Program. One of Howard Hendricks' classic and memorable lines to me was, "Don't you know that it's easier to change people's theology than it is to change their schedule or Program?"

Key Question: How will we program effectively to accomplish Christ's Purpose in the lives of these people?

Priority #4 – PROPERTY

Property is the ***tools*** we use. A person in telemarketing may not be able to function without his computer and appropriate software. A roofer cannot put on roof on a house without his hammer and roofing nails. But the tools are not the business of the telemarketer or the roofer. Property is what we have to have to get the task accomplished. Tools are essential; we can't do the job without them. They are on the priority list, but they are #4.

Key Question: What kinds of tools and facilities will be necessary to provide the Programs to help people move toward Christ's Purpose for their lives?

Priorities and Pentecost

In Acts 2, the first priority was to fulfill the commission Christ had given the disciples.

- **P-1 Purpose** . . . They declared openly that Jesus Christ who was crucified was both Lord and Christ (v. 36)
- **P-2 People** . . . The people accepted the message, rented, believed and were baptized, and suddenly there was a church of 3,000. That's church growth! (vv 38-41)a
- **P-3 Program** . . . Imagine Pastor Peter and Elder John asking, "Now, what are we going to do with all these people?"

  Verses 42-47 of Acts 2 give the ABCs of how Jerusalem First Church translated their Purpose into an ongoing Program.

  Here's how they did it: they devoted themselves to . . .

  - **Apostles' teaching** – instruction from their leaders
  - **Fellowship** – relationships with each other
  - **Breaking of bread** – focusing on Christ, and
  - **Prayer** – communicating with God

  The results were astounding!

- **P-4 Property** . . . They met together in the temple courts for larger celebrations, and they also gathered in small cells in their homes.

Priorities in Church History

PURPOSE. When you think of Purpose, what comes to mind? New religious movements throughout history have started with the mission or Purpose. Yet, within a few generations, often the driving passion of the Purpose gets lost and the organization or church becomes just a series of Programs. Is your Statement of Purpose more than a denominational document stuck away on a remote shelf in the pastor's study?

PEOPLE. When you think of people in relationship to the church, who do you think of first? . . . families who have been there for a few generations, or the people who are attending now, or the people who need to be there for Christ's sake?

PROGRAM. When you think of Program and church life, what comes to mind? In American culture, it is the Morning Worship Service; everyone knows it's at 11:00 o'clock. Do you know why? It's because it was the mean time between morning and evening chores in an agrarian society. There was a very logical reason for worshiping God at 11:00 o'clock on Sunday morning. People were able to do their morning tasks on the farm, then hook up the horse and buggy and ride for an hour or whatever time was necessary to get to the church. They had their service and then dinner together on the church grounds before returning home for their evening rounds of responsibilities. Yet there are churches in America that still seem to believe that 11:00 o'clock is the sacred hour.

Sunday School was born out of the vision of Moody Memorial Church in Chicago many years ago. They had a sense of mission to provide teaching about Jesus Christ to the unchurched children of the inner city. Yet it became part of the American tradition of church programs for children of churched families.

Sunday evening services began when very innovative pastors decided to use the invention of electricity as an evangelistic tool. With exciting new electric lighting, major churches (I believe, first in Chicago) decided to have evening services. People came to church out of curiosity and a lack of something better to do on Sunday evening, and many people made commitments to Christ. Sunday evening became a great evangelistic hour. It was an effective program in meeting and reaching people.

Wednesday night services found their roots in the agricultural society, as well. Christians felt the need to meet together with other believers during the week. They would gather in smaller clusters in homes nearer their farms after their evening chores.

All of these programmatic traditions, which had very healthy origins and were once effective in meeting people's needs, are poured in cement in some American churches today. The question is, are they still effective in reaching the people who are living at the end of this millennium?

PROPERTY. When you think of Property, what comes to mind? . . . the great cathedrals that dominate the skylines of many significant cities in Europe and America?

. . . the proliferation of community churches in America after the Second World War? What a wonder that the Church exploded across the Roman Empire and survived the first three centuries, often without any facilities.

I have been asked for years when Calvary Community is going to build a church. My answer is that I believe we *are* building a church. After 21 years, we were still meeting in leased warehouse buildings. We did need more adequate facilities in order to facilitate what God wants to do.

When facilities limit the capacity for ministry or lack the adaptability to accommodate new ministries, they can become Priority #1 by default.

Your Personal Church Priorities

Purpose • People • Program • Property

Think about your personal church experience. How were these Four Ps prioritized in the church in which you grew up? What received the most attention? I have asked this question when leading many pastors' and church leaders' seminars. Let me share the results from some of my informed surveys:

At a major pastors' seminar in Indiana, what do you think Midwestern pastors answered that question? Program got the most attention. They grew up seeing what the church does as the first priority.

In speaking to a group of Baptist pastors, People got the most attention. They grew up thinking church is who the People are and what they want.

At another conference, 48 respondents said Programs; 33 said People; 17 said Property; 1 said Purpose.

Sometimes the majority answer is Property. The church is the building. I have almost never heard people say the Purpose of the church received the most attention.

ASK YOURSELF . . .

In your personal church history, which of these four priorities received the most attention?

In your present church experience, which gets the most attention?

Get the Church's Priorities in Order

- **Purpose**: Why does Christ's Church exist?
- **People**: Who are the people we are uniquely called to reach out and serve?
- **Program**: How can Christ's Purpose happen in the lives of these people?
- **Property**: What kinds of facilities and equipment will be necessary to provide the Programs to help people move towards Christ's Purpose for their lives?

Differentiate Between the Changeless and the Changing

What is changeless? What must change? You may have grown up saying, "Two things never change . . . death and taxes." Now we live in a world where the one constant is change. Yet there are churches highly resistant to change—churches that are still saying, "We've never done it that way before."

Beccy and I remember going back to visit a church in Pasadena where I had served as youth and music pastor during seminary. It was 25 years later. The buildings were rundown and unattractive. Many of the older adults we had known in the congregation were still there, but the younger generation was missing. The same people were still in the choir, and the music was terrible. The order of service was essentially unchanged: there was no vitality or life. This was not a liturgical church, yet the liturgy had become poured in cement. They were still "doing church"—quite poorly, to be honest. As visitors, we stood out like sore thumbs. I think the people were shocked that someone new had actually come. We walked out hurting for a church that had at one time been so vital but had lost its vision and contact with the real world. Their Program hadn't changed. They were still doing church in the same way they had done church for decades!

Purpose is Changeless and Ageless

What facets of the church are changeless, and what facets are changing? . . . the answers are quite obvious when we think about it. The Purpose of the church finds its roots in God's Word. Christ and his Purpose are changeless. Essentially, his Purpose for the church has been the same in every age, the same from the first century till now. It is ageless and intergenerational . . . the Purpose Statement for Calvary Community applies to children, youth, adults, seniors. We may state it using slightly different terms and a more contemporary vocabulary, but God's Word and his intentions for the church are the same, generation after generation, world without end.

One of my **life lessons** was learned in my third year as a pastor. We were going to build our first all-purpose building at the little church in Orangevale, California, the church I had helped to launch. After berating other pastors for putting their noses into the building process, I found myself doing the same thing! I was even helping the designer, saying, "If I don't do it, who will?" I hadn't learned yet how to get past that question.

The morning came to dig the foundations for the building. I greeted the contractor excitedly, then I came back at noon to see what progress they were making. It appeared to me that the primary corner stake, from which they had laid out the trenches for the foundation, was too close to the property line. I went into my office and took a look at my set of plans. With a good eye and a tape measure, I did my own measuring during the lunch break. Sure enough, they were 10 feet too close to the property line, which would have been a violation of codes. After lunch, I had a discussion with the contractor, who said, "I'm sure it's fine." After 15 minutes of extended conversation and my insisting, "Let's measure it again," – sure enough, it was 10 feet off.

You know, it doesn't make any difference how well the rest of the building would have been built, it would have been all wrong if the foundation was wrong.

Life Lesson JESUS CHRIST AND HIS PURPOSE ARE THE CHANGELESS CORNERSTONE

Get this foundation for building a church right—or it's all wrong! **MAKING MUCH OF JESUS CHRIST must be the changeless focus for the church**. Paul, in 1 Cor. 3:11, says, "For no one can lay any foundation other than the one already laid, which is Jesus Christ." In Ephesians 2:20, he speaks of the church as *"being built on the foundation of the apostles and prophets, with Christ Jesus himself as the chief cornerstone."*

People change

But what about people? We all change; that's obvious. I remember showing pictures of Calvary's history in a Celebration. When the picture of me with a full head of curly black hair and a fairly healthy beard came on the screen, the place broke into hysterics. I looked more like the con artist Angel on the "Rockford Files" than the loving, founding pastor Calvary Community! People change. You don't think it's true of you? Look at a picture of you or your family from five years ago, or share your driver's license photo. Everyone laughs.

Ask the people in your congregation to describe their priorities and lifestyles in contrast with their parents' priorities and lifestyles: they are probably dramatically different than what they grew up with.

Program must change

People's needs are constantly changing, because their lifestyles, work, interests, and families are shifting. In light of the fact that people change, Programs must adapt and change to continue to meet needs.

Property needs will change

As Programs change, our Property needs dramatically change. We have moved into a technical/visual age, and the effective church must use technical/visual equipment. I recall visiting a large church that had screens in the balcony, with larger-than-life images of the praise leaders and pastor. As I looked around, I noticed that the people who were 30 and under were watching the screen; others were watching the people on the platform. The younger part of the audience grew up with TV as a primary companion and teacher. They felt more comfortable watching the screen than the actual person on the platform.

Avoid the Consequences of Violating Priorities

VIOLATION #1: Putting people first instead of Purpose

Many churches would say that people come first in the church, but they say it in different ways. It is natural to our nature to want to be first. It's the congregational meeting, where people feel they have a right to decide in a democratic way what ought to happen in the church. It's the strong pastor, who conveys that he knows best. Churches that put people first ask wrong questions: What do the people say? What do the people want? What does the pastor want?

I remember saying, in my early years as a pastor, "The kind of music I want in my church is . . ."

Recently, in a Celebration at Calvary Community, we were singing, "In our church, Lord, be glorified." I felt compelled to stand up, stop the singing, and say, "Let's change the words of that song. It is *not* our church; it is *his* church." In your church, Lord, be glorified." From that point on, whenever we sing that song, it represents a specific message to us. The Lord, Jesus Christ, and his Purpose come first.

A church will not find its vitality until it recognizes clearly and passionately that Jesus Christ and his Purpose come before people. But people are more important than Programs.

VIOLATION #2: Putting Programs first instead of Purpose

With time and tradition, Programs become sacred. If Purpose is not the changeless, driving passion of the church, Programs will be poured in cement. Programs are not sacred. Christ's Purpose is. Many churches fail to distinguish between Christ's Purpose and the Program to accomplish that Purpose.

Let me illustrate. Prayer is a critical function of the Church. Wednesday evening prayer meeting is a Program. It may be an effective means of Body prayer—if it isn't, change it! Prayer is sacred. Wednesday night prayer meeting is not.

VIOLATION #3: Putting Property first instead of Purpose

When are we going to church? We still refer to the church building as "the church." I remember asking a former congregation, "If something happened and this building were totally destroyed, would the church still exist?" It is easy to place too much attention on the church building. It happens through extended building programs and the pressure for building funds, which can be interpreted by the congregation as . . . "the building comes first." It is essential to articulate that we are building to have more effective ministries, not building to have a nicer facility. The building takes priority when our primary concern is the protection and care of the building, rather than the use of the building to facilitate ministries. Property is necessary—actually, it's essential – but buildings and tools must serve the Program needs. Put Property in its proper place.

There will be new life and vitality for the church when it gets its **Priorities in Order:**

PURPOSE	WHY?	WE EXIST
PEOPLE	WHO?	WE ARE
PROGRAM	HOW?	WE DO IT
PROPERTY	WHAT?	WE USE

APPLICATION QUESTIONS:

1. As I look at my personal church history, which of the Four Ps received the most attention?
2. As I see my present church, which priority gets the most attention?
3. What steps would it take to re-order our church priorities?
4. Who needs to own them?

Let clear priorities release your church to its full potential for Christ.

7

PRIORITY I: PURPOSE

Why? (We Exist)

Christ and His Purpose for His Church

The single most important question a church can ask is: *Why does Christ's Church exist?* Or, to be more specific, *What does Jesus Christ, the Head of the Church, want to accomplish?*

A. Catch Christ's Purpose

Jesus Christ made purposeful statements regarding his intentions for his church. In John 8:12, he said, *"I am the light of the world"*; but in Matthew 5:14, he said, *"You are the light of the world."* Christ's aim was that his followers would become a new source of light to this dark world. *"Let your light shine before men, that they may see your good deeds and praise your Father in heaven."* (Matt. 5:16)

In Matthew 16:18, he gave the open declaration of his intentions, *"I will build my church,"* and in verse 19 he tells the disciples he is passing the keys to his kingdom on to them. Does that create any images for you as a parent?—passing the keys to the new car to your 16- year-old and saying, "I'm giving you the keys and turning you loose."

Christ, after his last day of teaching at the Temple, confidentially shared with the disciples, "*And this gospel of the kingdom will be preached in the whole world as a testimony to all nations, and then the end will come.*" (Matt. 24:14)

In Matthew 28:19 is the command to the disciples, "*Therefore, go and make disciples of all nations.*" Had you been sitting there as one of his disciples, how could you have even imagined that happening . . . he was not just telling you to go to some people who were your friends, but the implication was to go change the world. Jesus spoke about the kingdom of God over 100 times in the Gospels. It was his favorite topic.

When anticipating an exciting event, how many times have you said, "You just wait!"?

Dr. Luke gave us Christ's last words on earth in Acts 1. It was as though Christ said, *because I am leaving Jerusalem, don't you leave. You just wait!* He told them to go back and wait for the gift that had been promised—the Holy Spirit. (v. 4) The disciples preferred to ask questions about restoring the Kingdom. Jesus said, in so many words, it's none of your business what the time schedule is, but I'll tell you what your business is: "*You will be my witnesses in Jerusalem, and in all Judea and Samaria, and to the ends of the earth.*" (v. 8) And these were his last words. Can you imagine how mind-boggling it was for the disciples, when, ten days later, in one day, the church exploded on the world—3,000 strong?

B. Catch Our Marching Orders

Have we caught these mind-boggling concepts?

- we are to be the lights of the world
- he's handed us the keys
- we are to give testimony to the whole world

If you want to start a business, you first must decide what you want to accomplish. The task of church leaders is quite different. We must first clearly discern what Christ wants to accomplish. We catch his marching orders. We don't create them. It is our task to:

Clarify his Purpose

- Commit our lives to it, and
- Communicate it continually.

1. Clarify Christ's Purpose.

On Sunday, November 2, 1975, when a nucleus of 21 members voted to rebirth Calvary Community, literally the first priorities were:

- **BIBLICAL OBJECTIVES:** (1) That the Biblical Objectives of the church be clarified and established in writing.
- **OUR COMMITMENT:** (2) That the pastor and board recognize Jesus Christ as the Head of this church and commit themselves to the Biblical Objectives as the basis for future planning and decision making.

We didn't know, as yet, what that statement of Biblical Objectives would actually include, but we did know that once we clarified what we thought the Bible said the church was to be, that had to be the absolute priority, the basis for all planning, and the primary grid against which the church board would make all future decisions.

We established a Christian Reformed tradition at Calvary. That is, whenever the elders meet or we have a leadership retreat, we place a Christ Chair at the head of the table or in the center of the room. We begin by acknowledging Jesus Christ's presence and that we are there to accomplish his purpose and will. That is our primary agenda.

Everyone has their ideas about the church. Clarifying the Statement of Purpose is the basis for having a united sense of purpose about Christ's Church. Get it off the shelf—it can no longer be a statement in the pastor's library from several generations ago, in words not recognized or understood by the people currently in the congregation. It must be Christ's Purpose, and it must be said in a way that the people can clearly understand.

2. Commit to Christ's Purpose.

When was the last time you sat in a board meeting discussing an important issue, and the question was asked, "How does this relate to our Biblical Purpose and our mandate from Christ?" You might more frequently hear, "How are people going to respond?" or "How will this impact our budget?" or "What is your opinion?" Our first question must be, "What is Christ's Purpose for us?" The operation of the church is not based on what the pastors or leaders want, but on what Christ wants. Have you seen the wrist bands that say, "W.W.J.D." (What Would Jesus Do)?

This can be all very theoretical, or it can move from the head to the heart and become a driving passion to motivate leaders to claim Christ's Purpose for their community. Visit a church that is dynamically alive, and ask people what their church is about. They may say it with slightly different words, but they will talk about their Purpose. In a vibrant church, people have caught the sense of Purpose that drives it. Visit a church that is not being effective or showing much vitality, and you may well receive 20 different answers from 20 individuals regarding what their church is about.

To commit to the Purpose means that it becomes Christ's mandate for the church. It becomes the drumbeat, the marching orders, the sense of higher calling and commitment. It becomes the basis for all planning and programming. Strategic and Program plans must be designed with Purpose in mind.

Purpose becomes the template for prayer for our community. As we prayed about what Christ would like to see happen and as we worked on the Purpose Statement for Calvary Community, something happened inside each of us. There was a new burning, a new appetite, a new mandate. There was a must. Jesus had told his disciples in Matthew 16:21 that he must go to Jerusalem and ultimately die as our Salvation. We said we must cooperate with him to see his salvation take place in our city.

The Biblical Purpose needs to be personalized in the life of each person who attends the church. That is Christ's calling for them as individuals as well as for the church as a Body.

3. Communicate Christ's Purpose Continually.

There is no greater motivation than the love of Christ and being captivated by a vision of what he would like to accomplish. Start asking Purpose questions:

Don't ask: "What would we like to see happen in our church?"

Ask: "What would Jesus Christ like to see happen in his church?"—"in our town?"

"Who are the people he would like to change?"

"What would he like to see happen in their lives?"

"How would he like to make this church different?"

Don't ask: "Would we like to see this church grow?" (You might get an honest "No!")

Ask: "Would Jesus like to see it grow?"

Don't ask: "What's most important to us about the church?"

Ask: "What's most important to him?"

Don't ask: "What kind of music do we like in our church?"

Ask: "What kind of music will help believers praise Christ and draw unchurched people to him?"

Don't ask: "What do we think we need?"

Ask: "What does Jesus think we need?"

Ask: "What would make us more effective in accomplishing his purpose?"

These are not the kinds of questions I heard asked in the church when I was growing up, nor are they the kinds of questions I hear very frequently now. To see an ineffective church become effective, to see a terminally ill church tum around and discover the miracle of new life, it takes more than thinking up new proposals and planning strategies. It takes a heart passion that comes from Christ about his passion for his church and his will for people.

As a leader, how can you help your people through a process that will lead them to arrive at a clear Statement of Purpose that can capture their hearts and captivate the spirit of the congregation? When Christ's Purpose becomes your driving passion, the will to change will happen. Purpose, instead of the Program, will become the cement of the church. As Christ changes people's hearts about the intentions of his church and the need for their neighbors to come to Christ, he will also change their attitudes about what the church does and needs to do.

Some of you may be asking, "How do we break the bonds of traditionalism?" Don't fight the Program or criticize it. But don't tolerate an ineffective Program either. The issue is not Program; the issue is Purpose.

Frequently I ask people who are new at Calvary, "Do you know the Purpose of Calvary Community?" Most people who have been there a few times can already share the four key words. Why? Because we communicate them continually, in ways that are understood by the churched—and the unchurched, as well. It's not enough to say the leaders know it. Do the people know it? What does that mean? At Calvary we communicate our Purpose in as many ways as possible; we

- celebrate it,
- say it,
- see it,
- repeat it.

Our Purpose Statement is visible on four major banners at the front of our Celebration Room. Symbols and the four basic key words are printed on most of the literature about the church. It is taught in orientation classes. It is shared at a Church Chat we have with people who are new to Calvary. It is referenced in teaching. It is brought up during Celebrations as we focus on some part of it. Our staff is organized around it. We set goals by it.

Purpose is the essence of Christ's intentions for his Church. It is at the heart of our very existence.

The Calvary Community Church Purpose Statement

Why does Calvary Community Church exist? What does Jesus Christ, the Head of the Church, want to accomplish in this church?

The Calvary Community Church exists to . . .

Celebrate the Life of God Eph. 3:20-21

Who?	*"Now to him who is able"*
To do what?	*"To do immeasurably more"*
Beyond what?	*"Than all we ask or imagine"*
How?	*"According to his power"*
Where?	*"That is at work within us."*
To whom?	*"To him be glory"*
Where?	*"In the church and in Christ Jesus"*
How long?	*"Throughout all generations, for ever and ever! Amen."*

Rev. 4:11 *"You are worthy, our Lord and God, to receive glory and honor and power, for you created all things, and by your will they were created and have their being."*

We are here to celebrate God's glory in the church, in this generation as much as in the first generation. As Jesus was growing up, for him and for other Hebrew children, the most exciting time of the year was going to the Temple for celebrations and festivals in the name of their Lord. Hebrew worship was an exciting, energizing, exhilarating experience, as people lived in tents made of twigs and spent a week in Jerusalem celebrating their God and his goodness. I've come to the conclusion that Hebrew worship was more like the Rose Parade than many typical American worship services.

I took a survey of over 100 people, asking them what came to their minds when someone said, "Worship Service." The first answer was, "boredom," quickly followed by "routine," "tradition," "sleep," "habit." Eighty percent of them gave a negative response. What a travesty that in our American culture many people cannot imagine anything more boring or mundane than gathering at a church for worship. This must make the heart of God ache. What a contrast is the Old Testament heritage of people parading with musical instruments and dancing, making their ascent to the Temple for their Holy Day celebrations. What a contrast to the dynamic life of the church as described in Acts 2, after Pentecost. This is the reason we call our weekly gathering together "Celebrations"!

Celebrate the Life of God . . .

A. Through awareness of and response to God's presence

Acts 2:46 *"Every day they continued to meet together in the temple courts. They broke bread in their homes and ate together with glad and sincere hearts, praising God."*

John 4:24 *"God is spirit, and his worshipers must worship in the Spirit and in truth."*

1 Cor. 1:31 *"Let the one who boasts boast in the Lord."*

When God's people come together for Celebration, his intention is that we become aware of who he is and respond to his living presence. His desire is for us to come with truth and integrity in our minds and a right spirit in our hearts.

Celebrate the Life of God . . .

B. Through Communion and commitment to Jesus Christ

1 Cor. 11:25-26 *"This cup is the new covenant in my blood; do this, whenever you drink it, in remembrance of me. For whenever you eat this bread and drink this cup, you proclaim the Lord's death until he comes."*

Col. 1:18-19 *"And he is the head of the body, the church . . . so that in everything he might have the supremacy. For God was pleased to have all his fullness dwell in him."*

God's intention is that Jesus Christ be the center of attention in everything that happens in the church. We come together to "make much of Jesus Christ." If someone walks into a Celebration only once, our prayer is that they will leave saying, "Jesus Christ is obviously the V.I.P. at this church."

Which member of the Trinity should get the most attention in the church?

It is the Father's will that the Son receives the supreme attention.

Celebrate the Life of God . . .

C. Through oneness and praise in the Holy Spirit

Rom. 15:5, 6 *"May the God who gives endurance and encouragement give you a spirit of unity among yourselves as you follow Christ Jesus, so that with one heart and*

> *mouth you may glorify the God and Father of our Lord Jesus Christ."*
>
> Rom. 15:13 *"May the God of hope fill you with all joy and peace as you trust in him, so that you may overflow with hope by the power of the Holy Spirit."*

God expects the church to be enduring, to be a center of encouragement, and to have a spirit of unity, so that our praise can be authentic. He wants to fill the church with joy and peace and overflowing hope. The Holy Spirit is the one who generates these relationships, the one who motivates our praise, the one who gives us a sense of unity. Isn't it amazing that all kinds of people come together from all kinds of experiences, and yet they are united together in praise and excitement about God? That is the work of the Holy Spirit.

These verses and concepts about Celebration have given us a focus to our prayer and a template for Celebrations. It doesn't mean that it always happens, but it does mean that the Purpose is clear. My prayer, before every Celebration I lead, is:

> "Lord, may the people be moved from the preoccupations of their minds to a mind set on you and a desire to respond with joy and praise to you.
>
> God, may people become aware of the fact that you are very much alive.
>
> Jesus, may you be clearly recognized as the V.I.P. here.
>
> Holy Spirit, bring joy, peace, unity, and overflowing hope to this God event."

The word "Celebration" means to come together in festive recognition of a person or an event. The goal is that weekend

Celebrations clearly focus on the person of Christ, and that every Celebration be an event rather than a predictable routine.

We exist to . . .

2. Cultivate Personal Growth in Christ

Eph. 4:11-13 *"It was he who gave some to be apostles, some to be prophets, some to be evangelists, and some to be pastors and teachers . . . so that the body of Christ may be built up until we all reach unity in the faith and in the knowledge of the Son of God and become mature, attaining to the whole measure of the fullness of Christ."*

Matt. 28:19-20 *"Therefore go and make disciples of all nations, baptizing them in the name of the Father and of the Son and of the Holy Spirit, and teaching them to obey everything I have commanded you"*

2 Tim. 2:2 *"And the things you have heard me say in the presence of many witnesses entrust to reliable men who will also be qualified to teach others."*

There is no clearer definition of Christian maturity than Paul gives in Ephesians 4. Being mature is being like Jesus Christ . . . reflecting his character. It's obvious that through Christ's life and ministry he accepted people where they were and expected them to grow.

The Epistles provide pictures of believers in the process of growing up to be like Christ. The church must not be a place where we reject people because they don't do it all right. It must be a place where we accept people based on their faith in Christ and expect them to change to be more and more like him.

Cultivate Personal Growth in Christ:

A. Through study of Bible doctrine.

"They devoted themselves to the apostles' teaching." (Acts 2:42)

If we do this . . . *"Then we will no longer be infants, tossed back and forth by the waves, and blown here and there by every wind of teaching."* (Eph. 4:14)

The basic beliefs handed down from the apostles must be clear in our minds and solid in our convictions, so that we won't be tossed back and forth by the winds of strange doctrine. This must happen in our churches, so that young people who go away to university don't throw their faith overboard during their first semester.

B. Through application of Biblical principles to life

"When they saw the courage of Peter and John and realized that they were unschooled, ordinary men, they were astonished and they took note that these men had been with Jesus." (Acts 4:13)

"Do not conform any longer to the pattern of the world, but be transformed by the renewing of your mind. Then you will be able to test and approve what God's will is—his good, pleasing and perfect will." (Rom. 12:2)

The goal is not cognitive Christianity, but Christlike living; not the accumulation of information, but the application of God's Word to life, in such a way that people will see the reflection of Jesus in their lives. The goal is not Bible knowledge, but changed behavior. We must teach people to think like Christians if they are going to act like Christians. This is a process. God wants to see people develop to the point that they will stand the test and discover how good his will is. It's pleasant. It's always right.

To this end, I taught a series titled, "You'd Better Believe It!"—a study of Calvary's core beliefs—basic doctrine.

C. Through development of mature Christians who reflect the character of Christ.

> *"So that the body of Christ may be built up until we all reach unity in the faith and in the knowledge of the Son of God and become mature. Speaking the truth in love, we will in all things grow up into him who is the Head, that is Christ."* (Eph. 4:12,15)

The task of the church is to get people knowing and growing. The bottom line is changed lives. When I ask people what has happened to them since they have come to Calvary, the answer I hope to hear is, "I'm changing. God is changing me." Thank God, frequently that is the answer.

We exist to . . .

3. Care About One Another in Christ

> *"Just as each of us has one body with many members, and these members do not all have the same function, so in Christ we who are many form one body, and each member belongs to all the others. We have different gifts, according to the grace given to each of us."* (Rom. 12:4-6)

> *"Accept one another, then, just as Christ accepted you, in order to bring praise to God."* (Rom. 15:7)

"We proclaim to you what we have seen and heard, so that you also may have fellowship with us. And our fellowship is with the Father and with his Son, Jesus Christ. But if we walk in the light, as he is in the light, we have fellowship with one another, and the blood of Jesus, his Son, purifies us from all sin." (1 John 1:3,7)

Christians are a family. Often, in the Early Church, the only family that believers were left with was their family in Christ. I've walked into singles groups at Calvary and heard people say, "This is my family." During the Christmas season I feel deeply moved by this Purpose when I hear people say, "My relatives are all back on the East Coast, but I've come to regard these friends in my group, or others at Calvary, as my family. They're the people I'm going to be with during the holidays."

How does this caring about one another in Christ happen? A healthy relationship with the Lord will be revealed in healthy, loving relationships with one another.

Care About One Another in Christ:

A. Through sharing one another's joys, growth, and needs

"They devoted themselves to . . . fellowship, to the breaking of bread and to prayer. (Acts 2:42)

"Every day they continued to meet together in the temple courts. They broke bread in their homes and ate together with glad and sincere hearts, praising God and enjoying the favor of all the people. And the Lord added to their number daily those who were being saved." (Acts 2:46,47)

"Carry each other's burdens, and in this way you will fulfill the law of Christ." (Gal. 6:2)

As you read through the Acts and the Epistles, you find the believers sharing their joys, sharing what they were learning and where they were growing, and sharing their needs. They evidently enjoyed one another; they got together daily in each other's homes.

Care About One Another in Christ:

B. Through recognition, development, and use of gifts of the Spirit by every believer

> *"So in Christ we who are many form one body, and each member belongs to all the others. We have different gifts, according to the grace given us."* (Rom. 12:5-8)

> *"Now to each one the manifestation of the Spirit is given for the common good. All these are the work of one and the same Spirit, and he gives them to each one, just as he determines."* (1 Cor. 12:7, 11)

It is God's desire that every believer finds his way to make a difference in the lives of others who are part of the family. They need to give, as much as others need to receive. The discovery and development of spiritual gifts, as well as the deployment of ministry. are vital to the life and health of the church.

Care About One Another in Christ:

C. Through service and sacrifice to meet each other's needs

> *"All the believers were together and had everything in common. Selling their possessions and goods, they gave to anyone as he had need."* (Acts 2:44, 45)

> *"So that there should be no division in the body, but that its parts should have equal concern for each other. If one part suffers; every part suffers with it; if one part is honored, every part rejoices with it."* (1 Cor. 12:25, 26)

Surprise! Giving is not just for those who have the spiritual gift of giving. Giving is a natural and healthy part of caring relationships. God's intention is that the family not only shows concern, but also responds to the needs of others in the family. I recall walking into a singles' group, "to be their speaker" for the evening. The Lord said to me, forget what you have in mind to share; try listening. I thanked them for inviting me and decided to ask them a few questions.

"I'm so pleased that you feel welcomed here. How many of you have experienced divorce?" With some reluctance, 68 out of 74 people in the room raised their hands. "Could you tell me, please, what hurts the most?" For the next hour I listened as people began gradually to open up and to talk about the hurts, the pain, the consequences, many of which I had never even thought about. It was one of the great learning experiences of my life, and it was a great night of learning for them, as well. They learned that the family of Christ is a place where you belong, not only when all is going well, but also when life is not going well at all. That night, people left knowing that I, as the senior pastor, thanked God for them and that Calvary was a place that cared about people's needs and hurts. The motivation for that night came from this Statement of Purpose: We may not always be a caring community, but at least we know we need to be.

We exist to . . .

4. Communicate Christ to the World

"Therefore go and make disciples of all nations." (Matt. 28:19)

"You will be my witnesses in Jerusalem, and in all Judea and Samaria, and to the ends of the earth." (Acts 1:8)

We discussed for a long time if communicating Christ to the world should come after Celebrating, Communicating, and Caring, and we concluded emphatically, yes. The church must first be a healthy body of believers who are learning to be aware that the Lord is there, who are vulnerable in experiencing healthy growth and change, and are learning to care about each other.

As this happens, we have something significant to share with others and there is integrity and credibility when we share the Good News of life in Christ. Jesus doesn't say we should be witnesses, he says, we will be. We must be.

Communicate Christ to the World:

A. Through penetration of society

"Praising God and enjoying the favor of all the people. And the Lord added to their number daily those who were being saved." (Acts 2:47)

"All except the apostles were scattered throughout Judea and Samaria, Those who had been scattered preached the word wherever they went." (Acts 8:1, 4)

"Always be prepared to give an answer to everyone who asks you to give the reason for the hope that you have. But do this with gentleness and respect." (I Pet. 3:15)

Since the founding of Calvary Community, I have often thought and prayed Acts 2:47: "May the day come when Calvary will have a favorable impact on the entire community." As a matter of fact, based on this part of our Purpose, our five-year goal was that half of the people in the community would hear about Calvary Community and have a positive response to it. It was the people, not the apostles, who became scattered throughout Judea and Samaria, as though God had shaken his salt shaker in the area surrounding Jerusalem. Those salty young believers began to share who Christ was in their new neighborhoods.

Communicate Christ to the World:

B. Through reproduction of our life in Christ by evangelism

> *"Go into all the world and preach the good news to all creation. Whoever believes and is baptized will be saved."* (Mark 16:15,16)
>
> *"You will be my witnesses in Jerusalem."* (Acts 1:8)

Just as, when a doctor first talks to an expectant mother, his first concern is her health; so also, in the church, it takes healthy, growing believers to see healthy evangelism happen.

At Calvary Community, apples have become the symbol of healthy reproduction. When apple trees are healthy and they are together with other apple trees, apples happen. If the trees get adequate exposure to sun, nourishment, and water, the exciting fragrance of apple blossoms will fill the air. The-winds blow and cross-pollination takes place, and eventually, in due season . . . APPLES!

I doubt that apple trees fret about their ability to reproduce apples.

When Christians receive adequate exposure to the light of the Son of God—that's Celebration! When Christians receive healthy nourishment through the Word, and water what God is planting in their lives—that's Cultivation! When Christians experience the fragrance of God's love, and the cross-pollination of learning to love each other and care about each other's needs—that's Caring! Then the result will be fruit—APPLES—that's Communication!

One of the most exciting Celebrations we experience all year is on the first weekend in January. We have an Apple Celebration when we honor the people who came to new faith in Christ during the past year. We welcome them, congratulate them, and spend the entire service talking to them about their changed lives. We have bushels of apples all across the front of the platform, and at the conclusion of Celebration, I challenge people to expect natural fruit from their lives. In an Apple Parade, each person is encouraged to take an apple and go back to his or her seat for our "biting benediction." We all crunch into our apples simultaneously . . . letting the juices flow . . . getting a taste of the excitement of healthy fruit . . . thinking about the creative power of God . . . and expecting reproduction in our own lives as a natural byproduct of our celebrating, cultivating, and caring together. By the time we leave that Celebration, everyone has been deeply moved with the excitement of new birth.

A husband and wife who operate a large construction supply company believed that God would give them apples, and . . . it's happening! Within the last two years, half of the people who work for them have become Christians, as several share together in a Bible study group.

A lady who grew up in a pastor's home, attended a Christian college, and was experiencing a marital breakup, shared

God's strength in helping her face her problem with a friend who rode to school with her. That friend is now new in Christ, takes meticulous notes from Bible studies, and is teaching several other friends. She has become one of Calvary's evangelists and experiences much fruit.

A hospital administrator meets with his key personnel once a week to study leadership principles from Nehemiah.

A gentleman came to Calvary and made his commitment to Christ and to the Body. He said, "In the last six places in town where I've installed new business equipment, I've met someone who's talked about their experience in Christ and their growth through Calvary Community. I finally decided that what I was looking for in life must be here. After 16 years of not walking in the door of a church, I came to find out what they're all talking about!"

Three men in a new-Christians group believed together that God would help their sons to find Christ. Recently, in a baptism service, those three sons were baptized together.

Almost every weekend, people are interviewed during the Celebrations, sharing what God is doing in their lives. This sharing helps people to identify practical ways in which God can use them to win others, and it keeps the expectation levels where God would like them to be.

Communicate Christ to the World:

C. Through discipling by celebration, cultivation, and caring

*"Teaching them to obey everything I have commanded you. And surely I am with you always, to the very end of the age." (*Matt. 28:20)

When someone is new in Christ, what do they need?

People new in Christ need to experience the first three Cs. They need to learn to celebrate the fact that God is alive and alive in them. They need to learn how to cultivate growth; to be growing, developing believers. They need the care and love of the community. As that happens, they become healthy, reproducing believers. We Christians should expect to be effective witnesses in our environment.

Evangelism, communicating Christ to our world, is not a replacement for healthy church life, but the healthy fruit of church life. We are given the mandate in John 15 to bear much fruit, and to find great joy in it.

How Do I Write a Purpose Statement?

I'm glad you asked. When Calvary Community was reborn, we began with a series of weekly Bible studies. Everyone was welcome, and most of the 25 people in the church came, including the older children and teens. Ground rules were quite simple:

1. **We made a list of key biblical principles for church life:**
2. **We looked in the Gospels at passages where Christ talked about what he wanted to do in the world.**

Matt. 5:13-16	Matt. 9:35-38
Matt. 11:28-30	Matt. 16:15-29
Matt. 22:36-40	Matt. 24:13-18
Matt. 28:16-20	Mark 10:43-45
Luke 4:18-19	Luke 4:43-45
John 4:21-24	John 10:14-18; 26-30
John 13:34-35a	John 15:1-19
John 17:6-21	John 20:21

3. **We looked in the Book of Acts at passages about the development of the Early Church.**

   Acts 1:4-8 Acts 2:36-48 Acts 4:32-35
   Acts 5:42 Acts 6:1-7 Acts 8:1-4
   Acts 9:31 Acts 11:19-30 Acts 12:1-19
   Acts 13:1-3 Acts 14:21-28 Acts 15:1-4; 22-35
   Acts 20:17-38

4. **We looked in the Epistles at key passages where the church is the subject.**

   Rom. 12:1-6 Rom. 15:5-13
   1 Cor. 1:27-31 1 Cor. 3:16-17
   1 Cor. 12:4-7; 11-28 2 Cor. 5:17
   2 Cor. 6:1 2 Cor. 6:14-18
   Gal. 5:13-15 Gal. 6:1-10
   Eph. 1:19-23 Eph. 5:8-21; 23-32
   Eph. 2:19-22 Eph. 3:14-21
   Eph. 4:1-7;11-16 Col. 1:17-20
   Col. 1:24-28 Col. 3:15-16
   1 Thess. 1:3 1 Thess. 5:11
   Heb. 10:23-25 Heb. 13:7, 17
   Heb. 13:15-21 1 Pet. 2:1-5
   1 John 1:3-7 1 John 4:7-21
   Rev. 1:5-10 Rev. 4:11

5. **Everyone was encouraged to participate in the process. Each Bible study group looked at a few passages and simply asked:**

   a. What does this passage teach us about our relationship to Jesus Christ?

   b. What does this passage teach us about our roles as individuals?

   c. What does this passage teach us about our relationship to one another?

   d. What does this passage teach us about our relationship to the world?

As people studied these passages, they came up with certain recurring principles that are vital to the life of the church and Christ's Purpose. Then, a task force took these principles and formulated them into a clear Statement of Purpose.

Key Questions:

1. Does your church have a Purpose Statement? In what form?
2. Is it clearly understood and stated in the language of the people?
3. How committed are you to it? In what ways do you show your commitment?
4. In what ways does the Statement affect church-board decisions, organizational planning, weekly services, etc.?
5. How is it primarily communicated?
6. How many different ways is it communicated?

If you see that you need to write a Purpose Statement:

1. What would be the appropriate process for your church?
2. What are the primary obstacles?
3. Who are the appropriate people?

Clarify Christ's Purpose

- **Commit to Christ's Purpose**
- **Communicate Christ's Purpose Continually**

Since initiating this particular process of developing a clear Statement of Purpose and making it visible, **Calvary Community's Purpose** has been stated in four large banners in front of our Celebration Room. They are an integral part of who we are and what we are about. We now know of churches all over the world who display Purpose banners when they meet together to praise God. Here are what some churches have developed:

- Praise God for His Life and Love
- Produce Personal Growth in Christ
- Provide for One Another in Christ
- Proclaim Christ to the World

Calvary Evangelical Free Church; Simi Valley, CA Pastor Steve Brewer

- Magnifying Christ
- Maturing in Christ
- Ministering for Christ
- Multiplying Christ's Harvest

Rocky Peak Church; Chatsworth, CA Pastor David Miller

- Exalt God the Father, Jesus Christ, and the Holy Spirit
- Establish a Caring Community of Believers
- Equip Believers for Effective Service
- Extend the Kingdom of God in Amsterdam, the Netherlands, and the World

Crossroads International Church; Amsterdam, Holland

- Praise God for His Love and Mercy
- Prepare One Another For Works of Service
- Provide Love and Care
- Proclaim Christ Across the Street and Around the World

Crossroads Community Church; Camarillo, CA

- Praise and Glorify Jesus Christ
- Produce Personal Growth
- Provide A Caring Community
- Proclaim Christ to the World

Christ Church of the Valley; Palmdale, CA—Pastor Rod Allee

- Celebrate the Life of God
- Care About One Another In Christ
- Condition Personal Growth and Service
- Communicate Christ in Everyday Living

Coast Hills Community Church; Aliso Viejo, CA—
Pastor Dennis Bellesi

I recall sharing the need to compose a Statement of Purpose at a pastors' seminar. One pastor called me a week later, very excited. He said, "I did it! I just finished it. I spent the entire week studying key passages about the church, and I've written a wonderful Purpose Statement. I can't wait to take it to my church board next week!"

Leaders of the Body need to buy into the entire process. In the army, if you get too far in front of the troops, you might be mistaken for the enemy!

Have you watched a band march in a local parade? If the drumbeat stops, it's total chaos.

We had the joy of a personal interview with Ronald Reagan in his office. He was so gracious and personable. A story he told regarding leadership is about a lesson he learned when he was in high school. He was the drum major leading his school band. He recalls thinking that the music was becoming more and more muted. Quickly glancing back over his shoulder, he realized that he was proudly parading down the street by himself. The band had turned a half-block back! He learned that a good leader is sure the drumbeat is clear, but he also keeps his eye on the people he is leading. Critical to healthy church life and healthy church leadership is having a very clear statement of Purpose that is understood by the people, with encouragement to be committed to it, and communicated continually.

LET CHRIST'S PURPOSE BECOME THE CLEAR DRUMBEAT OF THE CHURCH

PRIORITY II: PEOPLE

Who? (We Are)

Who are the people we are uniquely called to serve and reach?

The church must be driven by Christ's Purpose; not by people. The key questions that govern the church must never be . . . what does the pastor want? or what do the people want? But the question must be . . . what does Christ, the Head of the Church, want? In many churches there are those intimidating tomcats . . . lay leaders with lots of power and clout, who know what they think ought to happen and have influence to bring it about. The pastor who leads with integrity must be tenacious in seeing that Christ's Purpose dominates the life of his church.

Some churches advertise or promote themselves as "A People-Centered Church" . . . what a travesty. Part of the decline of mainline denominations during the last forty years is the result of giving themselves to what they considered the "people agendas" of our society: What were people talking about? What did people want to hear? I believe people come to church to hear what God has to say about life.

Some of the most broadly recognized advertising of the last few decades was the Hertz -Avis tension: when you're #2, you want to be #1. When you're #2, you try harder. The same tension exists in the church—it's natural to want to be #1. No. Christ comes first. I frequently tell people at Calvary, "There is Someone far more important than you around here." It's not the pastors or the elders or the soloist or even a guest . . . it is Jesus Christ. At Calvary, people will always be #2 . . . Jesus must always be #1! The good news is, we are #2 in the priority list. Christ gave his life for people. People are far more important than any program or property.

A. Jesus Christ Was a Student of People

Christ understood people. Have you noticed how frequently in the Gospels it indicates that Jesus knew what was in the hearts of people?

> In Matt. 12:25, we read of Jesus regarding the Pharisees, *"Jesus knew their thoughts."*
>
> The story of Jesus healing a paralytic and forgiving his sins is recounted in Mark chapter 2: the teachers of the Law were sitting nearby. *"Immediately Jesus knew in his spirit what . . . they were thinking in their hearts."* (v. 8)
>
> In Mark 12:14-15, the Pharisees and the Herodians were trying to catch Jesus in his words, and they asked, *"'Is it right to pay taxes to Caesar or not? Should we pay or shouldn't we?'"* But Jesus knew their hypocrisy. *"'Why are you trying to trap me?'* he asked."

Christ accepted people. As you observe the Gospels carefully, you will notice that on several occasions the disciples were shocked at Christ's acceptance of people—the woman at the well in Samaria and the woman who touched his garment. Children came to him with their parents, wanting his blessing. To the disciples, these people were an intrusion on Christ's more important agenda. But Jesus was indignant and irritated with his disciples. He said, "*Let the little children come to me, and do not hinder them, for the kingdom of God belongs to such as these.*" (Mark 10:14) What does this say to us about how approachable Jesus was . . . how accepting he was of people? Children were not an intrusion to him. He graciously welcomed them.

I've discovered that part of loving and accepting people is loving and accepting their children. When families are leaving after a Celebration or an event with their children, I make it a standard practice to speak not only with the adults, but to crouch down and have a brief conversation with the children, as well. Church needs to be an accepting environment for everyone.

Christ expected people to change. A woman caught in adultery was brought to Jesus.

He asked her, "*Woman, where are they? Has no one condemned you?*" "*No one, sir,*" she said. "*Then neither do I condemn you,*" Jesus declared, "'*Now go and leave your life of sin.*" (John 8:1-11)

Jesus accepted her without condemnation, but he expected her to change; and there is every reason to believe that she did change. Jesus came and gave his life for people. His intention was to accept them where they were, based on his grace, love, and forgiveness; and to see them be changed and transformed by the power of that grace, love, and forgiveness.

B. We Must Be Students of People

Seek to understand people. We must be lifelong students of people. One of the greatest potential liabilities for church leadership is getting out of touch with people. We must master the art of being people watchers. I love to have discussions with people who do not know me and do not know my profession. It is far easier to understand where they are and how they see life, when communication isn't clouded by their preconceived ideas of a "pastor."

How do we become students of people? We need to be aware of the demographics and sociologic resources available to us regarding our communities. But beyond all of that, we must become great listeners and identify specific ways to learn about people.

We have a Church Chat once a month, when Beccy and I invite new friends at Calvary to our home. We always ask a pastor and wife and an elder and wife to attend, plus a couple of staff members. Why? It is one of those environments where God gives us the opportunity to be students of people. We gain insight into the kinds of people who are coming in the front door of Calvary; and the wonderful stories we hear about life change are incredibly motivating and encouraging. After some informal mingling and conversation, I usually ask two questions: *"What brought you to Calvary Community?"* and, *"Why did you decide to come back?"* I am continually amazed at how people openly and courageously reach right past those questions and share the hurts of their lives that brought them back to church. They do it because it's safe, it's okay, and they have been given permission to share. Typically, someone says, "Well, to be honest, I've gone through one of the most painful times of my life and thought it was about time to try to reconnect with God. I went to church when I was a child. . . ." Or, as someone said recently, "My husband is an agnostic and I thought I was too, until. . . ."

I have concluded that people do not decide to come to church because life is terrific, everything is going fine, and church would be a neat thing to add to their portfolios. They decide to come to church because of some traumatic change or need in their lives. It drives them to look for some outside help.

In order to get to know your congregation, how about doing some simple surveys in the church? We frequently ask people to answer some quick questions that help us understand who are attending Celebrations:

- How frequently do you attend?
- What age group are you in?
- What do you like best about Celebration?
- What concerns or suggestions do you have about Celebration?

Accept people where they are. *"Accept one another, then, just as Christ accepted you, in order to bring praise to God."* (Rom. 15:7) We must accept people where they are, rather than where we wish they were or they wish they were. Frequently I tell people . . . "Sorry about the tough stuff in your past; sorry about where some of you are. Isn't it wonderful that Jesus accepts us where we are, rather than where we wish we were?" If we are going to reflect Christ's love, that's where we start. We must accept people, but . . .

Expect people to change. The other side of Church Chat is that I share very openly the Purpose Statement of Calvary—the

Four Cs—and Christ's intention for their lives. I say, "This may not be a church where you'll feel very comfortable with what is taught at times, but you will hear what Christ's intentions are and what he would like to see happen in your life. You will be challenged to change. Wouldn't it be something if a year or two from now you could say you are very different than you were when you came, and that Christ's Purpose, these 4 Cs, are happening in your life?" We often end up praying over those who volunteer needs in their lives where they desperately need God's help. People leave Church Chat excited . . . they've shared and been listened to . . . they've experienced an accepting environment . . . they've been challenged to change. After the crowd goes home and Beccy and I are cleaning up the leftover

popcorn and punch, we always talk with amazement about how open, how vulnerable, how receptive people are, and how much they desire for Christ to make a difference in their lives.

C. Identify Three People Groups

Consider these people groups: the pastor, the people in the church, and the people in the community you feel called to reach.

Pastor. Who are you—socially, economically, educationally? What's your community orientation; did you grow up in a small town, a large city, the East, the Midwest, the South, the West? What kinds of people do you relate to best? Who do you enjoy being with the most?

Describe the person you would like to have for a life friend.

People in the church. Who are the people in the church? Have you done a survey recently to determine who they are, what age groups they are in, occupational orientations, backgrounds, incomes, what they read, what kind of music they listen to, etc.? What is the "pastor compatibility factor"? In other words, do the pastor's style, approach, convictions, passions, attitudes, and goals match the culture of the church?

People in the community we feel called to reach. Who are they? Where do they live? How much alike or how different are they from the pastor and the people in the church?

Pastor, look at yourself and your past. What unchurched people have you been effective in reaching?

Part of my decision to come to Thousand Oaks, California, to pastor Calvary Community, was recognizing that the nucleus of people in this community is very similar to the people I was being effective in reaching in Fort Wayne, Indiana. Many churches are stuck because there isn't a match between the pastor and the community; or the match is very poor between the people in the church and the people in the community you've felt called to reach.

I was sharing some of this in a Doctor of Ministries program at Talbot Seminary a few years ago. About half the pastors in my class quickly realized that they were very different from the people they were seeking to reach, and that they were probably in the wrong place to be effective as pastors! That was not exactly the result I had anticipated, but several of them made pastoral changes in order to become more effective, based on understanding themselves and their communities better.

We realized when I came to Calvary that the nucleus of people in the church and the people in the community we felt called to reach were very dissimilar. That is why we established the first-year goal to reach 15 families who would be representative of the community as a core for launching the new church.

Who are the people you are trying to reach? What do they do? When are they accessible? What do you think they need? What do they think they need? What sources have you looked at to discern who typical Joe and Joan Pagan are in your town? It is very important for a church to seek to identify the typical person they are trying to reach. We don't broadcast this or announce it to anyone. If people come who don't fit that typical grid, of course, they are very welcomed; but we know who our target market is.

Remember, when people first come to church, their initial questions are not theological; they are cultural. A young couple walks into church for the first time with a new baby, looks around and says, "Do we see any other parents of newborns who were up most of the night and are as tired as we are?" The Gen-X person who comes for the first time will probably be there because a friend has invited him, but he looks around to see how many of the people there are in his life stage. He looks at how they are dressed and asks, "Do I really fit here? Do I want to be here?" The person who has just gone through a divorce may walk in and look around to see if there are other people who look like they are there alone.

Everyone who visits says to himself or herself, "Is this a place where something is happening?" Probably within the first five minutes, people form an initial opinion. "I'm curious." "I'm interested." "Maybe this is a good thing for me." Or they tum off and have decided, "It's not happening here." "How soon can I get out of here?!" People very quickly form a positive or negative response to what's going on.

D. Remove Barriers and Build Bridges

Barriers. Warren Wiersbe, former pastor of Moody Memorial Church in Chicago, used to describe so graphically the "Fortress Church" mentality: the church that builds a moat around itself to defend its members from the evils and ills of the surrounding community and culture. This church becomes very effective at distancing itself from people and may even take pride in doing so.

A primary task of an effective church is to discover the barriers that are hindering or discouraging people from being a part of the Church.

As we become students of people, we are more aware of their needs, and some barriers become obvious. However, if the barriers aren't conspicuous to you, just ask people, "What intimidates you and keeps you from coming to church?" They'll tell you!

Identify the barriers and get them out of the way! The fact is that one out of three unchurched people would attend church if invited by a friend.

If your unchurched neighbors were to visit your church, would the barriers keep them from coming back? How do you think they would respond? What might tum them off? Is your church a rejecting or an accepting environment? Is attending church helpful, or is it dated and unrelated to where people live? Is it a "down" atmosphere, or is it "up"? What keeps church members from inviting visitors? One of the main barriers keeping people from attending church is their preconceived bias that worship services are "mundane and boring." The church's largest bridge to the community is accepting, exciting, creative, expectant Celebrations/Worship Services.

Bridges. We were in Seattle visiting some churches to observe what they were doing to be more effective. We decided to go out to a special restaurant to celebrate our friend's birthday. The restaurant is across the bay from the city, with a marvelous view. We discovered that there are two bridges to the peninsula where the restaurant is located. One is a new, modem bridge, high and well connected with the main highway south of downtown Seattle. Somehow, we ended up on the old bridge, which was low and not clearly marked, with complex entrances and exits and sharp turns. It had not been repaved in a very long time. We made it to the restaurant, but it was sure a bumpy, slow process.

I thought about churches and their need to build new bridges to people; new bridges that are easily accessible from the primary highway where people are traveling in their lives.

What are the primary bridges we are building to where people are in our community? A church that is effective in reaching people and leading them toward Christ's Purpose has built bridges that are greater than the barriers. People come because of some identified, felt needs in their lives: needs for relationships and friends, voids in their lives caused by broken relationships, hurts they have carried from bad experiences many years before, desires to meet some healthy people. Some people are wondering where the God is they left 20 years ago.

While Calvary was meeting in the restaurant, we showed a series of family films produced by James Dobson. After the Celebration, one man came out absolutely livid. He said, "This is unethical. I can't believe you would do something like this. I came here today at the advice of our family therapist, thinking this was going to be a lecture or presentation on family life. Instead, I discovered I'm in a church!" I profusely apologized to him that he evidently had not been told that the film was being shown in a church, and I thanked him for coming. After he walked away ten steps, he came back with quivering lips and a very humble heart. He said, "Everything I said is true, but I have to tell you, I have never been in a place where I felt so much love." Well, you know what happened. It wasn't long before he and his family knew the love, acceptance, and forgiveness of Christ.

Thank God that in today's society people recognize that they are coming apart and that they need some help putting life together. They recognize that they are out of glue in our crazy society, and that Christ may be, in fact, the crazy glue that helps them build something strong enough to hold life together.

A starting point for deciding how to reach people is:

1. Recognize the barriers that keep people from coming to church and start removing them.
2. Identify immediate felt needs in people's lives and build new freeway bridges designed to connect with those needs.

In time, people will become receptive to Christ and will become open to help with their eternal needs.

A divorce often means not only a divorce from marriage but also a divorce from church, as well. Our divorce recovery program has become one of the primary new freeway bridges to connect people to Calvary and Christ. The word is out. Calvary is the place to go if you've come apart, lost your self-esteem, and are in despair about the nightmare of the divorce you have just been through.

"I've gone to Divorce Recovery at this church in Westlake Village, and it's helped me a lot." That message is out in our community, and people keep coming. The need is so apparent, so obvious. In a divorce recovery group last year, during the second week of the program the director said, "If you've come here because of the hurt and pain of a divorce, we're going to help you with that. You may have centered your hopes in a person and placed too many expectations on your marriage. The crucial need in your life right now is to identify Jesus Christ as your source of hope. Recognize that a relationship with him is life's most important relationship."

The immediate bridge that brought people was divorce and their pain. That bridge very quickly opened the door to the essential spiritual need of their life, to recognize Christ as their center of life and his values as the basis for building healthy relationships. Several people met Christ that night. It happens in every divorce recovery series.

Other bridges we have at Calvary are substance abuse recovery; Confident Kids—a program for kids with unique needs; cancer recovery; incest recovery.

One evening, I walked through one of the larger rooms in our Activity Center and saw a group of about 18 people meeting in the corner. As they turned and recognized the pastor's presence, I offered a cordial and general, "Hope you're having a good meeting; sorry I interrupted." After I walked through the room and approached my office door, one of the custodial staff met me with a look of shock on his face and said, "You just walked through that room. Do you know who's in there?" Certainly, I recognized some of the people. "Don't you know what that group is?" "No, I guess I don't." He said, "That's an incest recovery group."

My heart dropped with disappointment at my insensitivity and the potential embarrassment of my violating their confidentiality. Then my heart jumped with joy . . . isn't it incredible that this is a church where an incest recovery group can happen? I paused and thanked God that this kind of ministry can happen at a church like Calvary.

E. Create an Environment

We looked at many barriers, and we asked ourselves what the atmospheric conditions are where people are eager to come, and where they eventually will discover Christ's Purpose for their lives. A few years ago, on a visit to Hawaii, my wife and I saw a huge plant climbing 30 feet up into a tree in lush tropical gardens. I turned to Beccy and asked, "Isn't that the same kind of plant we have in our foyer at home?" She said, "Yes, it's a philodendron." "Why has our plant only grown 6 inches in the last three years . . . and look at this?!" Her answer was, "Environment." Is our church a healthy environment where people can grow into Christ's Purpose for them? Does the environment make people feel free and excited about inviting others to come?

Be a church that accepts people where they are, but that also expects them to grow and change. Let Christ's Purpose become the personal agenda for that change. Christ has a Purpose in mind for his church, and that Purpose is primarily about people. He died for people. He gave his life to see people change.

ACCEPT PEOPLE WHERE THEY ARE

EXPECT THEM TO CHANGE

APPLICATION:

1. **People Groups.**
   a. Describe culturally:
      - Who are you as a leader?
      - Who are the people in the church?
      - Who are the people in your community you feel uniquely called by God to reach?
      - How's the match?

   b. Who could best help you identify and understand these people?

   c. What sources and resources do you look to for help in understanding your cultural perspective?

2. **Barriers and Bridges**
   a. What are the primary barriers in your church to your community?

   b. What are the primary bridges from your church to your community?

3. **Environment:**
   a. What are five words that first come to mind that would describe the environment of your service last Sunday morning?

   b. What are five words you wish would describe it?

PRIORITY III: PROGRAM

How? (What We Do)

How will we Program effectively to accomplish Christ's Purpose in the lives of people?

A. Jesus Christ's Strategic Plan

Jesus Christ was open to teach all who would listen, but he selected a few whom he would disciple and called them to follow him. He had a very carefully developed strategy to prepare the disciples for the passing of the baton: He spent time with them, showed them, sent them out to do it, and ultimately shared his vision with them.

After the Caesarea Philippi retreat experience (Matt. 16:13-19), where his disciples confessed that he was the Christ, the Son of the Living God, Jesus told them the keys of the Kingdom would be handed to them. Then he clearly set his course for Jerusalem.

There is a change in the focus of his mission at this point. During the last weeks of Jesus' life, it is obvious that he had set his parting agenda. It's almost as though he had checked off a list of significant subjects he needed to cover with the disciples prior to his departure. Jesus' parting words in John 14 through 17 are about the disciples' relationship with him, about bearing fruit, about the ministry of the Holy Spirit, about intercessory prayer, about the great command to love the Lord and to love each other, and about a great future. *"Do not let your hearts be troubled. I will come back and take you to be with me."* (John 14:1,3)

B. The New Testament Church's Program

In Acts 6, we learn about the criticism and complaints that came against the Apostles. In Jerusalem First Church, the Grecian Jews felt their widows weren't being treated right. This led to a change of strategy with the appointment of a new team to make plans to meet the widows' needs. The result: The Word of God spread, and the numbers of disciples increased rapidly.

The program and strategy changed as the needs changed. Paul even went so far as to say, *"To the weak I became weak, to win the weak. I have become all things to all men so that by all possible means I might save some. I do all this for the sake of the gospel."* (1 Cor. 9:22, 23)

The people who needed to be touched by the Gospel were different in different places; Paul adjusted his Program or strategy accordingly.

C. Programming Principles

1. Christ and his Purpose must always be #1. It's ageless and changeless.
2. People age and change, therefore Program must change.
3. Program must always be the servant of Purpose and people, never the starting point.
4. Resist the temptation to be a Program-centered church. Pastor, watch out for the
5. natural inclination to go to a conference and come home with The Program.
6. Design Programs that will move people toward Christ's Purpose for their lives (i.e., the 4 Cs), programs for every age, stage, and people group in the flock, in light of their needs. Programs must be pragmatic. What works?
7. When the Purpose becomes clear, we begin to ask different questions about Programs:

Celebrating

- How can we help our people get excited about celebrating God's life?
- How can we help them remember that Christ comes first?

Cultivating

- What can we do to see that they're growing and maturing to become more like Christ?
- What kinds of Programs can help us best accomplish these Purposes Christ has in mind for their lives?

Caring

- How can we help them to express care about one another?
- What will encourage them to reach out and include their friends?

Communicating

- What gets in the way of people bringing friends?
- What are the barriers?
- How can we enlarge the bridges?

These questions need to be asked regarding each life stage, from infants to seniors.

The objective of the Program is to help people move toward Christ's Purpose for their lives. Christ clearly moved from obvious felt needs to essential spiritual needs. The day he fed the 5000 men was followed by the day he told them he was the Bread of Life. The first day, he gave them physical bread to meet their obvious felt need. The second day, he talked to them about their essential spiritual need: to experience him as the Bread of Life. (John 6:35)

D. Programming Process

Start with an evaluation of the felt needs of people. What are the needs they are feeling deeply about? How can those needs become the bridges to the essential spiritual needs, expressed in the four "Cs"? Let people be involved. Don't ask People to implement the Programs that leaders have designed. Allow them to participate in the process of developing those Programs. Every part of the Calvary ministry goes through the planning process on a yearly basis. Plans are put in place for September through the following June. As ministry teams begin to develop some strategies, there are essential questions to be asked in the planning process:

- **Evaluation.** What are the primary felt needs of these People?
- **Identification.** What are the three primary strengths and the three basic obstacles to this part of the ministry?
- **Brainstorming.** What are the kinds of Program possibilities or things we could do? What kinds of Programs would best help accomplish Calvary Community's Four Cs [or Christ's Purpose] in the lives of these people?
- **Purpose clarification.** How does this relate to the Statement of Purpose for the church? Which one of the Four Cs does a particular Program address?
- **Goal setting.** What specific goals could be accomplished? We usually seek to set a numeric goal, a leadership goal, and an outreach or evangelism goal.
- **Implementation Plan.** What basic steps are involved? Who will lead it; who will staff it; who will train for it? What leadership, staff, training, recruitment, communications will we need?
- **Schedule.** When and where will each step take place?
- **Resources.** What human resources and financial resources are needed?

- **Tracking.** Are we on target? Is it actually happening? How do we know it's happening? How will we keep track of it? Is there a report-back system?

I remember having a specific Program in place for contacting visitors. Visitor cards were sent to a group of people who were to make phone calls before the next weekend to thank the people who visited and encourage them to come again. In addition to this, a letter was to be sent. I went to the pastor who gave oversight to this and asked him how it was going. He said, "Fine, I'm sure. We have people in place to make those calls." I asked, "How do you know it's happening? How many calls are actually being made?" He answered, "It's all in place, and we have chosen faithful people to make those calls. I'm sure it's fine." I said, "Let's check." That's tracking.

We talked to the staff people who processed these visitor contacts. "Do you get reports back each week or each month to know that, in fact, calls have been completed?" "No, we don't think that's necessary," they answered. I told them, "Yes, it is necessary." Would you believe, we discovered that, for various reasons, during the last four months the callers had stopped calling . . . one because of an illness in the family, another decided they could no longer carry that responsibility, etc. Without tracking, a Program may not be happening, and we may not even know it.

- **Ruthless re-evaluation.** On a regular-basis, we need to stop and carefully evaluate every ministry of the church—I suggest annually. Once the Purpose for the church is clear, Programs can no longer be sacred cows. Programs at Calvary Community have been removed from the sacred throne they have occupied in many traditional churches. As a matter of fact, every Program must justify its right to continue and exist, based on only one thing: is it helping people to move toward Christ's Purpose? The integrity of the Program is its relationship to the integrity of Christ's Purpose. What's the grid for evaluation?

  1. What was the stated objective for this Program or ministry?
  2. Have specifically stated goals been achieved? If not, what has been accomplished?
  3. Are people, in fact, growing and developing and moving toward Christ's Purpose?

  After re-evaluation, the decision must be made to

  - **refine,**
  - **redesign,**
  - **replace,** or
  - **remove** that Program.

This is a question of pragmatics. What works, what will make it work better, what would work better in its place, or, is it really needed or necessary? This may sound very complicated, but it isn't.

Develop a conscious yet casual style of ongoing evaluation. Let me illustrate: I remember doing an informal evaluation of a Celebration during a Church Chat with a group of new people at Calvary. After talking about the "Four Cs" being the basis of Program ministry, etc., at Calvary, I simply asked them to think back on their weekend Celebration experience:

- **Celebration:** What happened at church to help you to really be aware that God is there? What pointed to Jesus Christ as the most important person there? Where did you see joy or unity or praise or hope through the influence of the Holy Spirit? They shared quite openly about it.
- **Cultivation:** I got up my courage and asked them to help evaluate my teaching. What basic teaching about Christianity did you learn? What principle did you learn that could make a difference in what you do tomorrow at work? How did the service help you to grow or change?
- **Caring:** What went on in the Celebration this weekend that helped you to feel that this is the church where people really care, or that showed someone caring for someone else?

Do you know what you can do to get connected with other people in the Calvary family?

- **Communicating:** What happened that indicated that unchurched people are welcome here, or that people were discovering who Christ really is? What might have caused a guest to feel threatened or turned off?

Involving people in evaluation is a simple process, but a very essential one.

E. Calvary Community's Programs

Our two essential programs are Celebrations that happen when we come together and Cells that happen at homes. These programs find their roots in Acts 2: The people met together regularly in the Temple courts, but also in homes. It seems apparent, in looking at The Acts, that the church got together and celebrated who Christ was with great joy, and they received teaching from the apostolic leaders. It is equally evident that much of the growth, development, sharing, and living out their faith happened in small groups in their homes day after day.

As a matter of fact, reflecting on Christ's ministry, he taught the masses, but he developed a dozen disciples. It's interesting today that sociologists have observed that the ideal maximum size for a group where people are growing and learning and personally involved is about 12. I certainly have the impression that Jesus was a good sociologist; don't you?

I am often asked, "How do you get people past their hang-ups about changing the Programs of the church?" Focus on Christ's Purpose until it becomes the driving passion. Help people see that Programs are only servants and must justify their existence, based on their effectiveness in accomplishing Christ's Purpose. Re-focus on this Key Question:

- **How will we Program effectively to accomplish Christ's Purpose in the lives of these people?**

PROGRAM MUST BE THE SERVANT THAT HELPS PEOPLE REACH FOR [OR EXPERIENCE] CHRIST'S PURPOSE

10

PRIORITY IV: PROPERTY

What? (We Use)

What kinds of tools and facilities will be needed to provide the Program to help people move toward Christ's Purpose for their lives?

A. Christ and the Early Church

Christ seemed to do his work anywhere and everywhere. He ministered in a natural amphitheater outside Capernaum; in a boat pushed out from the shore of the Sea of Galilee; outside the city gate at a well in Samaria; in the synagogue of Nazareth, where he grew up; at a private party in the house of Zacchaeus in Jericho; and at a city parade in his honor in Jerusalem. He taught on the Temple steps, in the Temple courts, and sitting on the Mount of Olives during his last week in Jerusalem. Wherever people came and whenever they would listen, he ministered to them. It seemed to be simply a matter of finding an environment that was effective.

We read in Acts 2 about the birth of the church. It is indicated, by the mass of people from all the different nations who heard and responded to the Pentecost message, that it happened in an open place where people were coming to worship. The activity of Jerusalem First Church continued in the Temple courts and in homes (Acts 2:46- 47).

In Acts, chapters 16 and 17, look at the variety of environments where you find Paul: In Philippi, it was down by the riverside—that's where the people were. It was also in the house of Lydia. It was in the city jail and at the jailer's home. It was in the Jewish synagogue, as was Paul's custom. It was in Jason's home in Thessalonica. In Athens, it was again in the synagogue with the Jews. Then it was in the marketplace, day by day, with whoever would listen. It was on Mars Hill, just west of the Acropolis, where the Greek philosophical elite met and discussed religion or morality—all with no Property ownership or payments!

In the first few centuries, Christianity exploded and penetrated much of the Roman world, with very limited Property. They met where they could, and they used whatever facilities worked.

B. Put Property in Its Place – #4 Priority

- **Tools are essential.** Whatever job you're doing, there are some necessary tools. A telemarketer sits in his office, but without appropriate phone equipment and his computer, monitor, and software, he is out of business. The tools of the church are: the facilities, equipment, parking lots, Bibles, educational materials, bookstores, visuals, sound equipment, lighting, furnishings, musical instruments, computers, etc.

We see Bibles as one of the primary tools people need to be reaching for Christ's Purpose in their lives. Therefore, we have a Bible Sunday annually and encourage people to purchase NIV Bibles. We have a variety of them available for purchase, but we also provide free NIV Bibles to anyone and everyone who wants one. We say that it is essential to have a Bible to grow in your walk with Christ. "We want you to have one. Go ask for a Bible, and it's yours!"

- **Tools are not sacred.** In traditional European ecclesiology or church life, church buildings are seen as sacred. I think it is human nature to have an affinity for and to feel security with the physical . . . to value it more than the spiritual. That same thing happens with church buildings. But they are tools, not temples. *"'Don't you know that you yourselves are God's temple and that God's Spirit lives in you?"* (1 Cor. 3:16)

  Jesus was clear, in saying to the woman at the well in Samaria, *"Believe me, woman, the time is coming when you will worship the Father neither on this mountain nor in Jerusalem. Yet a time is coming and has now come when the true worshipers will worship the Father in spirit and truth."* (John 4:21, 23). Christ prophesied that the places we worship will change; but that's not really the issue. The issue is worshiping with integrity and passion. It's not the buildings . . . it's *us. We* are God's temples!

- **Tools must be chosen based on Purpose, People, and Program.** When we began looking for facilities at the time of Calvary's rebirth, we asked, "Where do the people in this community go for city functions?" The answer was the Hungry Tiger Banquet Room at the Los Robles Country Club. So, that's where we met for four years. We asked, "Where will we able to carry out the Programs that will help our people reach for Christ's Purpose in their lives?" Our temporary locations were certainly not magnificent, but they worked.

- **Tools become aged and obsolete.** Are we using the same software we used three years ago? Are we using the same technology for sound and visuals in the church we used five years ago? If so, we're losing ground rapidly. I visited a church and walked into their center for children. As the children arrived, a large screen immediately caught their interest. The rooms were alive with visual activity centers. They felt at home because children in our culture today are so comfortable with media.

  Don't let facilities, foundations, and cement become the foundation and cement of the church. In many churches, we have the natural disposition to build the Program around our facilities, rather than fitting facilities to our Program.

- **Tools affect your effectiveness.** A pastor friend of mine, John Greenly, once shared with me when his church was entering a building program, "We have much more important things to do than build buildings; that's exactly why we must build buildings!" A medical doctor says, "We have more important things to do than invest in expensive new technical equipment; that's precisely why we must do it."

- **Limited tools limit our effectiveness.** Although tools are not sacred, we can hurt the spiritual cause God has in mind when our tools are inadequate and ineffective. At Calvary, we were caught in an inadequate trio of industrial buildings that were intended to be temporary tents. At first, they were functional, but we soon became very restricted by our lack of space for Celebrations, other Programs, and parking. Tools we use in the church, particularly buildings, can become Priority #1 by default when they're inadequate, or when they become too much of the focus of the life of the church.

  The more flexible the tools and Properties are, the better. With the rapid pace of change in our world, we will all struggle with investing in tools that too quickly become obsolete. We're asking right now what kinds of sound and video equipment need to be available to have effective ministries to teens. We're evaluating what kinds of technical equipment we need for Celebrations and for Christian education, now and into the next decades.

C. Calvary's Property Saga

When I joined the Calvary nucleus, they were existing in a modest little A-frame church that seated 120 people. The capacity would soon be confining. The location was on a side street in "Old Town." The identity was inappropriate. The ambiance was unsuitable. We asked what environment or tools would match the people we felt God had called us to reach in the Conejo Valley. We knew different tools were essential.

Where could we locate where new people would come? What facilities would not only accommodate people, but be visible, accessible, central to the community? We did not want to be a church just for Newbury Park, Thousand Oaks, Westlake Village, or Agoura; but a church for the Greater Conejo Valley. That meant staying on the freeway corridor . . . neutral turf. Every church that I knew of in the valley had a neighborhood-church mentality: We are the Baptist Church of Newbury Park, the Presbyterian Church of Westlake Village . . . that was the mind-set. The orientation we were praying for was to reach a broader segment of the people, and to break through the local community barriers to a sense of greater community identity.

We moved. We began meeting in the banquet facility at a local country club. It worked! Was it ideal? Hardly! We had to bring in a crew very early on Sunday mornings to air out and shovel out the remains of Saturday night's party. But there was a real feeling of camaraderie as we worked together to get the place decent and set up for Celebration. We had many funny moments . . . when the aroma of bacon or onions from brunch being prepared in the kitchen was almost more than we could bear, or when the piped-in music for the restaurant blared through our speaker system at the most inopportune times, or when the junior-high boys' Sunday School class got into the drinks in the bar (their Sunday School room!).

It was revolutionary to think of the church meeting in a country club. At the time, I didn't know of another church in the U.S. doing that, although I am sure there must have been some somewhere. I've already talked about Young Set Club, the best-known children's facility in town, where we held our Sunday School through 6th grade. These tools were very important, very essential.

In three years, we were looking for Property because we knew the restaurant would soon be obsolete. We made an appointment with the city planner, sat down with him, and asked him what was the most visible, accessible, central and large parcel of land left in this valley. We located that Property and, with only a handful of people, we purchased it for $400,000. Why? Because we felt an appropriate location, a larger tool, would be necessary for our future growth. This property was located at the intersection of the 101 and 23 freeways. We eventually came to the conclusion that the City of Thousand Oaks would never allow us to complete the project.

Within three years we were having two morning services at the restaurant. We were out of space and, because there was no room in the parking lot for people to come for the restaurant brunch, we were politely told to leave . . . in 30 days.

Again, we asked where there was a freeway-accessible parcel or building of some kind that would accommodate the people who were coming. Another aberration took place: we ended up choosing a warehouse. Did we know of anyone who used a building like that for a church? Not at that time, but that didn't daunt us.

How do you warm up a warehouse and make it look attractive? It was not a matter of a warehouse being an acceptable facility; it was a matter of adapting the industrial building, adding some visually aesthetic features to match the culture of the people we're serving. Fluorescent lights are not warm. Exposed warehouse ceilings are not attractive. A big rectangular box is not aesthetically beautiful. We attempted to make it feel less industrial by hanging large, colorful banners on the bare walls. To this day, we use banners to express with sacred art the subjects of my teaching series. The warehouse idea worked. Today, warehouse churches are common in the American Church.

One of the great things about our leased warehouse was the flexibility: being able to change the facility as the needs changed.

Soon it became—expand the room; push the wall back. Next it was: add a balcony and increase the seating capacity by 35 percent. After that, it was: lease additional warehouses for children, youth, and other adult ministries. Then it was: add a Saturday-night Celebration and lease another parking lot. One of our great liabilities was lack of adequate parking. We literally had only 40 parking spaces available to us!

I am happy to say that today we are occupying that new property we had considered along the freeway. We were suffering from what is called, in Church Growth terms, sociological strangulation. Our facilities had been inadequate too long. It caused a plateauing of attendance. People came because they really wanted to be there, in spite of the obstacles. My great concern was for the people who were being turned away, simply because there was no place to park, and there was nowhere to sit if they did manage to get in. The barriers were greater than the bridges to our facilities.

We had many difficulties and delays. Obtaining our building had become far too important, by default. The price tag for developing Property in California is astronomical, and it had seemed out of reach.

Finally, however, God helped us to get into another building. We are now occupying a large industrial office building—a relic of the Cold War. It seemed too large . . . at first . . . but that's the way we felt when we moved into our warehouse location. Our new-to-us building was an old, tired building, but it was refurbished and renewed. We took on a huge financial challenge. Some would say we couldn't afford it, but actually, we couldn't afford not to move.

The price is too great if we fail to accommodate the work God is doing. Leadership is claiming the land, like Joshua. Leaders must put their feet in the water, and watch God make a way!

We moved into our new campus in September 1998. This center of Cold War focus now became a center for preparing for spiritual warfare. Our goal was that our new campus would become a center for preparing people for peace—for the Kingdom of God.

> "Many peoples will come and say,
>
> *'Come, let us go up to the mountain of the Lord, to the house of the God of Jacob.*
>
> *He will teach us his ways, so that we may walk in his paths.' . . .*
>
> *He will judge between the nations and will settle disputes for many peoples.*
>
> *They will beat their swords into plowshares and their spears into pruning hooks.*
>
> *Nation will not take up sword against nation, nor will they train for war anymore." (Isa. 2:3,4)*

Tools are essential to see it happen. I remember being with Pastor Rick Warren when they had moved onto their extensive Property and put up a tent. I think the novelty of the tent made Saddleback Church even more appealing. I remember Rick telling me that as they added additional parking lots—the next week people came and filled them. The church literally grew and expanded based on adequate seating and available parking.

When God is at work and dynamic growth is taking place, the task of leadership is to accommodate what God is doing. Property is not sacred, but it sure accommodates God's sacred Purpose. Parking space isn't sacred, but it sure accommodates people who need to find God's Purpose in their lives.

I remember one Sunday, after we had moved to meeting in the warehouse location, I asked everyone in the Celebration who had come to the church and had met Jesus Christ in the last three years to stand. We were astounded as 40 percent of the congregation stood. People instantly applauded and thanked God for them. But I wanted to make a different point: "Would you please thank the people who were here, who had the vision and the spirit of sacrifice to reach for this larger warehouse building, while we were still meeting in a restaurant? If those people hadn't had the heart to make more space available, there wouldn't have been room for you to come."

Space issues? There were space concerns the day Jesus was born. Was there room in the inn? Room in the restaurant? Room in the warehouse? Room in the auditorium? Room in the classroom? We must make space available. We must make room to accommodate the spiritual task God wants to accomplish. In the future, perhaps more and more of the ministry of the church will happen in homes, in community centers and other facilities. In our rapidly changing world, flexibility and variety may well be the name of the game.

Property must accommodate the Programs that will help People reach for Christ's Purpose in their lives.

I've been asked since the day Calvary was reborn, "When are you going to build a church?" I always pause for about 10 seconds and say, "We have been building a church. Do you mean a church building?" The fact is, Calvary has reached thousands of people and, to this point, has not owned any buildings. Frequently, in talking with pastors who are about to plant new churches, my impression is that too high a priority is placed on building and owning buildings. The issue is not what tools do we own, but what tools are available? The task is to provide facilities, not necessarily to own them. It may well be that the greatest flexibility and most effective economy for the church of the future will be to not own any buildings, but rather to lease Property short-term. Find facilities and tools that work, and use them. Seek to adapt them or dispose of them when they become ineffective or obsolete in accomplishing the task.

CONCLUSION:

- God's Purpose is ageless and changeless.
- People are obviously aging and changing.
- Programs age and must change.
- Property ages. and Property needs change.

APPLICATION:

- **What are the primary tools we need to carry out the ministry God has given us?** Make a list of tools necessary to carry out each of our programs . . . buildings, parking, seating, technical equipment, visual equipment, etc.
- **How well do our tools meet our present needs; our projected needs?** How can we adapt our present tools; or what new facilities do we need to cooperate with what Jesus Christ is doing, and, in faith, to accommodate what we believe he's going to do in the future?
- **Where are we adapting Programs to serve the tools?**
- **In what ways do we communicate around the church that tools are not temples . . . just necessary implements?**

- **Have we asked people what gets the most attention around our church?**
  - Christ's Purpose
  - The People
  - The Program *or* —
  - Our Property

Whatever tools and facilities we have exist to serve the Program — to help the people move toward Christ's purpose.

SECTION D.

PRIMARY PRINCIPLES

11

PRINCIPLES—CORE VALUES

"The Heart of Who We Are"

In the rebirthing of Calvary Community, we identified four founding principles. The church must be:

- Christ Centered,
- Biblically Based,
- Culturally Relevant, and
- Outreach Oriented.

A. Christ Centered

At one point, our son, who is now an associate pastor in his own church, preached for the first time at Calvary Community. Beccy and I were in Seattle observing another church, but my mind was at Calvary. I watched the clock . . . not timing the service I was attending but anticipating the moment our son would get up to teach and the minute he would finish, as well.

Afterward, I said to Beccy, I was more delighted about Kirk teaching at Calvary today than if I had been there teaching myself. The week before, our daughter, Laurel, had sung at our Celebrations. I was more thrilled about her singing than if I had been doing it myself, and I know the congregation felt the same!

This is how it is, when Mom and Dad are cheering with excitement as one of their kids scores a goal in a soccer game. It is this way, when parents celebrate along the parade route as their child marches by in the band. It's the father and mother, bursting with pride and joy at a graduation ceremony.

I think that the human emotions of pleasure and pride we feel in seeing our children honored help us to understand the heart of God the Father. The Father's pleasure is to see his Son as the center of attention and affection. In Colossians 1—the magnificent passage about the supremacy of Christ in the Church—Paul writes,

> *"And he is the head of the body, the church; he is the beginning and the firstborn from among the dead, so that in everything he might have the supremacy. For God was pleased to have all his fullness dwell in him, and through him to reconcile to himself all things, whether things on earth or things in heaven, by making peace through his blood, shed on the cross."* (18-19)

It was John the Baptist who said, *"He is the one who comes after me, the thongs of whose sandals I am not worthy to untie."* (John 1:26) As the best man attends the bridegroom, so John the Baptist, Jesus' Best Man, states this passionate imperative to exalt Christ: *"He must become greater; I must become less."* (John 3:30)

Christ's own words, when describing the kind of death he would experience—being lifted up on a cross—were. *"I, when I am lifted up from the earth, will draw all men to myself."* (John 12:32) When we lift up Jesus Christ and his Cross, he draws people to himself.

Interesting, isn't it, that on the day of Pentecost (Acts 2), Peter faced his listeners with the issue of the Cross. *"God has made this Jesus, whom you crucified, both Lord and Christ."* (v. 36)

Again, in Acts 4, Peter and John were before the Sanhedrin, and they had the audacity to say the same thing: *"It is by the name of Jesus Christ of Nazareth, whom you crucified but whom God raised from the dead, that this man stands before you healed."* (v. 10)

Calvary Community was born with a deep conviction that we are here to Make Much of Jesus Christ; to lift him up, and to present his sacrifice on the Cross without apology. Paul clearly said, in 1 Corinthians 1:22-24, *"We preach Christ crucified: a stumbling block to the Jews and foolishness to Gentiles, but to those whom God has called, both Jews and Greeks, Christ the power of God and the wisdom of God."*

The Cross is not a palatable or even comprehensible message, yet Paul's challenge to us is to present the Cross of Christ to people. He was confident that God would reveal his power and show people the wisdom of following Christ.

Ephesians is the book, more than any other in the New Testament, that talks about the nature of the Church and speaks of God's Purpose in Christ:

> *"To bring all things in heaven and on earth together under one head, even Christ."* (1:10) *"God placed all things under his feet and appointed him to be head over everything for the church, which is his body. the fullness of him who fills everything in every way."* (1:22)

"To him be glory in the church and in Christ Jesus throughout all generations, for ever and ever! Amen." (3:21)

"Grow up into him who is the Head, that is, Christ." (4:15)

In Philippians, the result of Christ's humiliation will be his ultimate exultation:

"Therefore, God exalted him to the highest place and gave him the name that is above every name, that at the name of Jesus every knee should bow, in heaven and on earth and under the earth, and every tongue confess that Jesus Christ is Lord, to the glory of God the Father." (2:9-11) *Paul wrote this while in prison in Rome, where Caesar ruled and demanded the confession that "Caesar is Lord!"*

This Scripture established a new dogma that stood in the face of the demands of Caesar

. . . a new creed and personal greeting among believers, "Jesus is Lord!"

It was Dr. Warren Thompson, the senior pastor under whom I served as youth and music pastor while I was in seminary, who gave me my life motto when I asked him what advice he had for a young man starting out in his first pastorate. He simply said, "Be sure you make much of Jesus Christ!"

Life Lesson MAKE MUCH OF JESUS CHRIST

A founding principle of Calvary Community Church was that we would make much of Jesus Christ, without compromise or apology.

Calvary Community's Name

As we reviewed the name of the church, we decided to continue using the name that had recently been chosen, "Calvary Community.: The place of crucifixion—in Latin, called CALVARY—in Aramaic, called Golgotha—in English, called the Place of the Skull—was the place of forgiveness, salvation, and hope in Christ. We were to be a COMMUNITY of believers who come together based on what Christ did for us at Calvary, and we were here to impact our COMMUNITY.

A key Calvary prayer has always been, "May Jesus Christ be recognized as the V.I.P. whenever people come together at Calvary."

He owns the church. It's his Bride. He paid the ultimate price for her.

> *"I saw a new heaven and a new earth. I saw the Holy City, the new Jerusalem, coming down out of heaven from God, prepared as a bride beautifully dressed for her husband."* (Rev. 21:1,2)

Let everything revolve around Jesus Christ. He is the center!

B. Biblically Based

James, the brother of Jesus, was a skeptic until after the crucifixion and resurrection. He became the principal leader of the church in Jerusalem, and the New Testament's major proponent of faith that works. He said, *"Do not merely listen to the word, and so deceive yourselves. Do what it says."* (Jas. 1:22) He followed this with a humorous illustration: it makes no sense if a person looks in the mirror in the morning, walks away, and forgets what he sees and doesn't do anything about it. The purpose of looking in a mirror is to make the necessary changes in your appearance, as best you can. James' word of wisdom is: *"The man who looks intently into the perfect law that gives freedom, and continues to do this, not forgetting what he has heard, but doing it—he will be blessed in what he does."* (v. 25)

God's blessing and freedom will come as we seek to teach people not only what God's Word says, but what to do about it.

> *Changed lives: "Do not conform any longer to the pattern of this world, but be transformed by the renewing of your mind. Then you will be able to test and approve what God's will is—his good, pleasing and perfect will."* (Rom. 12:2)

Christian faith is a matter of being reborn in your spirit, renewed in your thinking, re-directed in your behavior. People must learn to think like Christ if they're going to live and act like Christ. His intention is to change our minds, our thinking. A metamorphosis is to take place; literally a transformation in the way we think.

To Calvary Community, being biblically based means being committed to a confidence that God's Word will be the effective source for changing the way people think and live. The Bible must be taught with a focus on life-change principles. We make a basic assumption: we expect God's Word to change people's lives. The primary evidence of God's work in the church will be changed lives. We seek to accept people where they are, but we expect God to change them.

C. Culturally Relevant

Jesus certainly was in touch with people. Part of the religious community's irritation with Jesus was their anxiety and jealousy about his connection with people, and their lack of connection

Paul, in 1 Corinthians 9:19-22, presents this principle: *"Though I am free and belong to no man, I make myself a slave to everyone, to win as many as possible."*

The goal is to win as many as possible to Christ. We need to approach people with great sensitivity to where they are: To the Jewish community: *"To the Jews I became like a Jew, to win the Jews. To those under the law I became like one under the law, (though I myself am not under the law), so as to win those under the law."* To the Gentile community: *"To those not having the law I became like one not having the law, (though I am not free from God's law hut am under Christ's law), so as to win those not having the law."*

Paul didn't alter the essence of the message, but he definitely tailored the style of his presentation to be relevant to a particular audience. *"To the weak I became weak, to win the weak."* He was very sensitive about offending people by his manner or personal demeanor. If people were offended, it was because of the message, rather than the method or manner of presentation.

CONCLUSION

"I have become all things to all men so that by all possible means I might save some." This means to us that **we must develop cultural awareness.**

The better we understand people, the more effective we can be in influencing them for Christ. We must build broader bridges, and we must address or remove the barriers. We must communicate in words people can relate to, rather than burden them with theological terminology or "church-eze." We need to use stories and illustrations that relate to their life experiences. Presenting Christ with relevance has to do with the total environment as well: the decor of the building and platform, the music, a contemporary translation of the Bible, language of the current day, even our dress.

When they enter our church, people new to attend church must not get the impression that they've walked into a sub-culture or are caught in the past. Jesus is relevant to people of every age, and we need to be sure that our environment communicates that to a person in his or her initial visit.

D. Outreach Oriented

In Acts 2, where the dynamic birth of First Church in Jerusalem is described, notice the finale . . . *"Praising God and enjoying the favor of all the people. And the Lord added to their number daily those who were being saved."* (v. 47)

The church was truly intimidating to the people of Jerusalem, who were steeped in Jewish culture and very aware of the scandalous crucifixion of Christ. Rather than focusing on the tension and conflict, Luke ends the chapter with the pleasure and good will God allowed the church to have with the Jerusalem community at large. "Enjoying favor" meant having a positive influence. And the result—the Lord added to their number daily those who were being saved.

The church must never lose sight of the fact that we're here to have a positive influence on our community; to see an ever-increasing number of people coming to terms with Christ and the Cross and discovering the new life he has in mind for them. We must provide a welcoming environment for newcomers; they need to feel like favored guests.

God graphically taught me this lesson on a summer vacation many years ago. The stark and vivid memory is still fresh in my mind. (I had grown a full beard while traveling, to be a bit incognito.) We chose to visit two small, traditional churches on the Sundays we were vacationing, one in Northern Michigan and one in Stratford, Ontario, Canada. In both of those services, with 50 or 60 in attendance each, we were conspicuously the only visitors there. At the end of each of those services, invitations were given, and it quickly became apparent that all eyes were on our family. People were praying earnestly that we'd make the break and come to the altar to receive Christ. I can't remember when I have felt more uncomfortable; we felt cornered, trapped. The pastor giving the invitation from the platform was looking solely at us, and we were squirming. Would you believe that at the end of the service in Michigan, I walked to the door and greeted the pastor. In shock and embarrassment, he recognized me as a fellow pastor, and he was tongue-tied. The Gospel and the message of the cross are not to be compromised, nor are they to be an embarrassment. The people in those little churches had a genuine desire to see others meet Christ. Yet their manner of extending the invitation left us feeling alienated and cornered, rather than included.

That experience left an indelible impression on me about the importance of helping unchurched people to feel welcomed; of being sensitive to the dynamics happening when they walk through the door of our church. We must balance our sense of urgency that people find Christ with great understanding and sensitivity toward the unchurched people in our community. What is it regarding churches that makes people apprehensive? It is about feeling uncomfortable and unacceptable . . . guarding their anonymity . . . not being hit up for money . . . not feeling pressured or manipulated.

I recall speaking to a man, who came out of Celebration one day and said, "This is my first time, and I feel OK about being here." "Oh, tell me what you mean," I asked. He said, "I was scared to death. I hadn't been in church in 25 years. It was really quite intimidating for me to just walk in here this morning, but I feel OK about it . . . I'll be back." I thanked him for his courage to tell me how he felt.

We need to be reminded that many people feel like this. He kept coming back, and soon he had made his commitment to Christ.

These were the primary assumptions with which we began the rebirthing process of Calvary Community. We believe an effective church must be . . .

- **Christ centered,**
- **Biblically based,**
- **Culturally relevant,**
- **Outreach oriented.**

We're as committed to these principles today as we were when Calvary Community began.

12

PRESS FOR THE MARK: VISION

Why Christ has Placed This Church in This Place at This Time

A. Christ's Final Vision

Christ's parting vision-casting was: *"You will be my witnesses in Jerusalem, and in all Judea and Samaria, and to the ends of the earth."* (Acts 1:8) He assured them that the Holy Spirit would come on them and empower them for the task. It's obvious that as Jesus was ascending back to heaven, his desire was to plant this vision in their thoughts and hearts. These words literally became the template for the Book of Acts.

B. Paul's Vision

In Philippians 3:12-15, Paul made a powerful vision statement about what he believed to be his life calling: *"I press on to take hold of that for which Christ Jesus took hold of me."* (v. 12) The words "to take hold" literally mean to apprehend someone.

Have you ever been arrested?! Why did Jesus Christ apprehend Paul? Why did he apprehend you or me? Paul enlarges on this thought:

1. Focus	"one thing I do"
2. Forget it	"Forgetting what is behind"
3. Fight for it	"straining toward what is ahead,"
4. Fix your eyes on it	"press on toward the goal"
5. Prize is heaven!	"to win the prize for which God has called me heavenward in Christ Jesus."

"All of us who are mature should take such a view of things." (v. 15)

C. Vision is . . .

- Vision is focused.
- Vision is singular.
- Vision lets go of many things and says, "This is the main thing."
- Vision is something for which to fight and give your life.
- Vision is a fix on the future.

The Purpose must be clear and clearly based on Scripture. As I said before, we will express the church's Purpose Statement with different words, but it is essentially the same for all churches in all generations. Vision answers a more specific question: Why has Jesus Christ placed this particular church in this community at this time?

Vision is at the foundation of all the dynamic work of God throughout time. When you look at your Purpose and your people and the uniqueness of your leadership, in prayer before

God, discover your Vision. Vision is: what you are called to do about what you believe.

God gave Haggai a vision of completing the building of God's house, which had been started 18 years before. *"Build the house, so that I may take pleasure in it and be honored,"* (Hag. 1:8) God also promised Haggai, *"I will fill this house with glory."* (Hag. 2:7) This vision became the driving force that caused Haggai to lead God's people, who had returned to the land, to finish the work on the Temple. The work had been stalled, through lack of vision and preoccupation with other, lesser matters. They completed the building in the next 42 years.

Solomon was very clear about the consequences of failing to cast a vision. *"Where there is no revelation, the people cast off restraint."* (Prov. 29:18)

Every leader must ask; every church must answer: Why has Jesus Christ placed this particular church in this community at this time? What's the main thing? What's our primary calling? What are we really all about? Can we say it in a nutshell? Can we state it in a sentence?

D. Calvary Community's Vision Statement

In the earliest days of Calvary's rebirth, the first vision statement was formulated:

> "to share Jesus Christ with relevance
> to develop a new form of church life"

We later enlarged it to say:

> "to share Jesus Christ with relevance—loving, accepting, and relating to the needs of people in this progressive and complex world to develop a new form of church life—based on the exciting principles in the New Testament and insights received through church-growth studies."

People must be inspired to claim the Vision. One special day, our people marched all over the parcel of Property we owned along the 101 Freeway. A plane flew overhead, and it was sky-writing, blazing numbers across the sky for the whole city of Thousand Oaks to see: "69661." At Celebrations the next week, I asked the people what "69661" meant. "It's about the square footage of the Property"; "the future address of the Property"; "the price of the Property"; and many more complicated and creative guesses. The right answer was that 69661 was the number of unchurched people in the Conejo Valley. It was symbolic of our Vision.

Re-Vision. We have recently reformulated Our Vision:

Why has Jesus Christ placed Calvary Community Church in the Greater Conejo Valley at this time?

"TO HELP AS MANY PEOPLE AS POSSIBLE TO BE READY FOR CHRIST'S RETURN."

The Vision is about people. The Vision is about God calling people heavenward in Christ Jesus. "*I press on toward the goal to win the prize for which God has called me heavenward in Christ Jesus.*" (Phil. 3:14)

Say your Vision in a sentence. Publish it. Keep it before the people. But also flesh it out. How can it happen? Give the breakdown. What does it actually mean? Here's how we broke ours down:

TO HELP AS MANY PEOPLE AS POSSIBLE TO BE READY FOR CHRIST'S RETURN:

I have come to believe that Calvary Community's calling is to faithfully serve at least a tithe of the Greater Conejo Valley: to help 10 percent of the people in our community to be ready for Jesus Christ's return. WOW! That represents 20,000 people and growing!

When I have shared this numerical part of the vision, some people have responded with excitement and anticipation; others have taken two steps back and their mental computers began doing rapid math. Some people have responded by trying to reinterpret the vision: "Pastor, you mean that all the churches in the Valley will reach 10 percent of the unchurched, don't you?" No. "You mean that 20,000 will walk through the doors at some time for a Program or activity, don't you?" No. "You mean 10 percent of the Valley will be touched in some way by the church, don't you?" No. Every other church in our community is here to help prepare the harvest, as well. It's for each church to sense God's personal vision for them and their place in harvesting; then we work together to see it happen.

Personally committed to Jesus Christ as Savior. How can we see as many people as possible personally committed to Jesus Christ as their Savior? As many people as possible actively following Jesus Christ as Lord?

How does that happen? Well, that's already been clarified; it's through the Statement of Purpose and the Four Cs and the People Pathway (which I will talk about in Chapter 14).

- **Celebrating** the life of Christ . . . being personally excited about and aware of God's living presence.
- **Cultivating** personal growth in Christ . . . People in process, growing, developing, changing, becoming more like him.
- **Caring** about one another in Christ . . . recognizing that they're part of the family.
- **Communicating** Christ to the world . . . our world: the people around us, the people we know, who need to know who he is and the difference he can make in their lives; and ultimately reaching out to communicate Christ all over the world.
- **Eagerly anticipating the return of Christ as King.** *"So you must also be ready, because the Son of Man will come in an hour when you do not expect him,"* (Matt. 24:44).

You must continually remind people—we are waiting for Christ's return!

"When's the big day?" We must help every believer to know —it's the day we are permanently united with Christ. It must become as much of an immediate response as that of a prospective bride, when asked about her "big day." She understands that the "big day" refers to her wedding day, when she is united with the groom.

The elders said to me, "You really believe God has given you this vision, and we have gone on record affirming it with you. The people have applauded it. BUT—how can it become *their* vision? It must be theirs if it is going to happen. How can the body grasp it, believe it, own it? This questioning led to the development of a bookmark that personalizes the vision for each member of Calvary. Rather than "Our Vision," it says, "My Vision."

I asked each person to list on their bookmark two people in each category: family, friends, neighbors, co-workers. I set a challenge before the people of Calvary to help them grasp the vision—2,500 people praying that 8 people will find salvation in Christ. 20,000 people being prayed for individually! Their challenge was to:

- **Pray regularly** for them by name
- **Be authentic** with them
- **Be available** to them
- **Invite them**—to a Celebration or to a special event
- **Share their story**—write it out
- **Share Christ's story**—a sentence, a brief conversation, or a booklet, like "Your Most Important Relationship"—however God opens the door.

Still, it seemed like we could do more to own the vision. At Calvary Community, we have a huge banner on our west wall that portrays our vision. What if we asked people to transfer the names on their bookmarks to that wall . . . using 6 inches only, no last names (to protect confidentiality)—and then have the congregation pray together for these named individuals to meet the Lord?!

We did it! Some call it "Calvary graffiti"; others say it's our "wailing wall." The number of names transferred from bookmarks to the wall keeps growing.

E. How to Help People Claim the Vision

- **Say the Vision—repeatedly.** Have the people declare it out loud in services.
- **Teach it regularly** in leadership classes and wherever people are learning about your church.
- **Print it**—in every bulletin and major publication.
- **Make it visible in Celebrations/Worship Services** – consider having a large Vision banner in your Celebrations Room.
- **Pastor: talk about it** with leaders and in small groups
- **Illustrate the Vision,** by having people share in your services stories of life change.
- **Personalize it** – help your people to own the Vision personally. "My Vision: To help as many of my friends as possible to be ready for Christ's return."
- **Pray about it** – in various environments and gatherings of the church.
- **Discuss it** in your small groups.
- **Celebrate it**—with new people who come to Christ.

When I look out over our Conejo Valley in prayer, I envision the growing Bride of Christ in this Valley.

> *"Then I heard what sounded like a great multitude , , , shouting, 'Hallelujah! . . . For the wedding of the Lamb has come, and his bride has made herself ready. Fine linen, bright and clean, was given her to wear."* (Rev. 19:6-8)

Let the Vision become the passionate prayer of the people!

13

PUT IT ALL TOGETHER

I was pastoring my first church in Orangevale, California. We were expecting our first child, and my wife, Beccy, was having an afternoon rest. I was in another room looking out the window, watching the wind blow as a winter storm approached. I saw the tree outside our bedroom where she was sleeping begin to crack and lean toward the house. I ran, flung open the bedroom door and yelled, without any explanation, "Get up and get out of here! Now!" She looked at me like I was crazy. As I shouted it again in desperation, she reluctantly, but cooperatively, left the room. At that moment, we heard an incredible crash as half the tree came down next to our bedroom. I learned something out of the shock of that experience.

Sometimes people are more responsive if we take time to explain our erratic behavior, but at times there may not be an opportunity for explanation.

A. Root Systems

The other thing I learned was that eucalyptus trees grow very rapidly with lots of top, but with very limited root systems. The deceptive consequences are that they're not as strong and stable as they look. The taller they get, the more vulnerable to storms they become. Most healthy trees have as much growth below the ground that's invisible as they do above the surface that's clearly seen.

We will do well to give a lot of attention to the root systems and the foundations for growing healthy, vibrant churches . . . churches that will stand strong and tall. The root system of most trees is not only equal in size to what's above the ground: it's also essential.

B. The Church Culture

Principles, priorities, purpose, programs, projected results . . . how do you "put it all together?" In our city, Thousand Oaks, California, oak trees are the primary symbol of our city; so, we chose to "put it all together" around the symbol of an oak tree. Find a way that's appropriate for you—an imagery, a way that pictures the essence and elements of your church. Get it all on one page.

- **Biblical Purpose**: Why do we exist? Without the primary roots of our biblical Purpose in place, there is not a basis for expecting a healthy church to grow. What will help people to experience God's Purposes for them individually and as a church family?
- **Core Values:** What are basic convictions that guide the behavior and ministry of the church you are part of? These convictions are an integral part of who you are.

Take them away, and the very essence of your church would be altered.

- **Vision:** Why has Christ planted this church in this place at this time? What do we feel uniquely called to be for Christ's sake? What do we feel uniquely called to do about what we believe? The congregation and leaders must become united with passionate prayer to claim the Vision.
- **Programs:** How will the ministry be facilitated? What kinds of Programs are necessary to see the church branch out and grow with strength and balance? What needs can we reach out and meet?
- **Fruit:** The fruit are the anticipated results as the beauty of Christ begins to reflect in the lives of the people. What will people look like? The ultimate evidence of healthy faith is reproduction of the character of Christ, as characterized in the New Testament by the fruit of the Spirit, and reproduction of new believers.

C. What Makes Calvary – *Calvary?*

What makes us who and what we are? The oak tree captures the essence of who we are. The:

- **Root Systems** – the essential convictions about our ministry, are summed up in our
- **Core Values** – Christ Centered; Biblically Based; Culturally Relevant; Outreach Oriented.
- **Trunk** – *Vision* – to reach people: to help as many people as possible to be ready for Christ's return. What we are called to do about what we believe.

- **Branches** – ***Ministry*** – Ministry programs: celebrations, cells, and other ministries.

How to facilitate the ministry:

- **Leaves** – ***Growth*** – Life change: each believer celebrating, cultivating, caring, communicating.

The anticipated results of ministry:

- **Acorns** – ***Fruit*** – Final evidence of healthy maturity—two kinds of fruit: The fruit of the Holy Spirit

New believers:

For us at Calvary, Acorns represent people who will potentially become strong Oaks of Righteousness.

> *"They will be called oaks of righteousness, a planting of the LORD for the display of his splendor."* (Isa. 61:3)

D. Suggestions for Getting It Together!

Now. put it all together for the church in which God has placed you. What makes you who and what you are?

- **Our Statement** of Purpose and our Core Values
- **Our Vision** – People
- **Our Programs** to accomplish Christ's Purpose
- **Our Fruit** – Evidence of life change and multiplication

GET IT TOGETHER: Clarify the essence and essentials of the church.

14

PEOPLE PATHWAY

> *"The Lord is my shepherd, I shall not be in want. He makes me lie down in green pastures, he leads me beside quiet waters, he restores my soul. He guides me in paths of righteousness for his name's sake."* (Ps. 23:1-3)

God is described as the Shepherd of his people 20 times in the Old Testament. Many of God's great leaders were shepherds: Abraham, Joseph, Moses, David, and some of the Prophets. To his disciples, Christ described people as "harassed and helpless, like sheep without a shepherd." (Matt. 9:36) He called Peter and the other disciples to *"take care of my sheep."* (John 21:16)

The most endearing term for a spiritual leader is "Pastor," which literally means "Shepherd."

A. Good Shepherds Lead

Jesus chose to describe himself as the Good Shepherd. He described the task of the shepherd: *"The sheep listen to (the shepherd's) voice. He calls his own sheep by name and leads them out. When he has brought out all his own, he goes on ahead of them, and the sheep follow him because they know his voice."* (John 10:3-4) *"Jesus used this figure of speech, but they did not understand what he was telling them."* (v. 6) The Pharisees listened to his words, but really didn't get it.

Do we get it? Often, when the sheep were sleeping, the shepherd was not only protecting them but also thinking about where they would go next. He anticipated the seasons. Where would they find grazing and water? He was aware of what they needed to grow and become mature. He had a personal sense of care and responsibility for them. That's what a shepherd's life is about. The shepherd/pastor is responsible to lead God's people. He goes first, and they have confidence in his care and direction. He calls his sheep to follow, and they do.

Dr. Peter Wagner, after a television show called "Faithways" that I did with him, said to me, "I think people want to follow their shepherd. They want to do the right thing. Have we made the path clear?"

B. Becoming Oaks of Righteousness

On Jesus' first return visit to Nazareth, his hometown, following his baptism and the launch of his ministry (Luke 4:16ff.), he went to the synagogue where he grew up and probably where he learned to read the Scriptures. He stood up and opened the scroll to Isaiah 61, choosing a passage that was a prophecy reflecting the nature of his coming and ministry. Jesus was making a statement to his hometown friends and family about how he would help people and where he would lead them.

> *"'The Spirit of the Lord is on me, because he has anointed me to preach the good news to the poor.*

> *He has sent me to proclaim freedom for the prisoners and recovery of sight to the blind, to release the oppressed, to proclaim the year of the Lord's favor.'"* (Luke 4:18-19); (see also Isa. 61:1-3)

He was the anointed one. His message would be good news to the needy, to a nation of people who were in conflict. He would bring recovery of sight for people who had lost perspective, and a sense of release to those who lived under a spirit of oppression. The time of God's jubilee had come. Continuing in Isaiah 61, he may well have read, *"'They will be called oaks of righteousness, a planting of the Lord for the display of his splendor.'"* (v. 3)

Ah, that certainly fits Thousand Oaks! The centerpiece of our community is oak trees. When you take a project to City Hall planners, nothing is more important than protecting our cherished oak trees. A shopping center was built in town, called "The Oaks," and a massive slice of the budget involved strategies for drainage systems, appropriate nourishment and intentional care of the oaks. Often, we are required to drive around the oak trees to find a parking space.

A 1940 census said there were 3244 oaks in town. By 1984, only 947 could be identified. In 1984, the suggestion was even made to change the name from Thousand Oaks to "947 Oaks"—the idea didn't fly; but a new emphasis on the importance of oak trees was born.

One of Calvary Community's associate pastors, John Hedegaard, pointed us to Isaiah 61:3, in 1982. God has called us to be *"oaks of righteousness"*: oak trees have character and exhibit strength . . . we have been *"planted by the Lord"*: God has put us here with a purpose in mind . . . *"for the display of his splendor"*: we're here to display the beauty of God in this community.

Today, when someone joins Calvary Community, they identify themselves as Oaks, planted by the Lord to display His splendor. Wouldn't it be something if, in the future, the Oaks of Righteousness planted by God—the members of his church—were every bit as significant to the life of this community as the oak trees themselves?!

C. The Path to Becoming a Mature Oak of Righteousness

1. BE PLANTED.

Celebrate . . .

- Celebration attendance—attend Celebrations regularly.
- Church Chat—at Pastor and Beccy's home
  – Get to know more about Calvary and about others.
- Commitment to the Body—God planted me in this church.
  – I commit to becoming an Oak of Righteousness.

- Beyond Church Chat—learn the ABCs of life at Calvary Community.

2. BECOME ROOTED.

Cultivate . . . Deepen your roots through a brief study of:

- Bible Doctrine
- Bible Study

- Sharing Your Faith
- Spiritual Gifts
- Spiritual Maturity
- Stewardship

3. **BRANCH OUT.**

   Care . . .

   - Connect to a small group for a time of sharing, support, study, and service with an extended family.
   - Commit to service. Every person needs to discover and develop their gifts and find their place to serve the Body.

4. **BEAR FRUIT.**

   Communicate . . .

   - Become a contagious Christian—we are all here to help our family and friends to get ready for Christ's return.
   - Connect to Christ's work in the world—support some missionary or project.

D. Suggestions for Developing a People Pathway

Once God's Purpose is clear, leadership needs to ask, what are the steps on the path? What is the track for people to take, to become who God wants them to be? Identify the sequence of steps. For instance, identify:

- **Entry point.** "I'm here!" Where's the front door to the church; how do they get here?

- **Assimilation.** "I'm feeling comfortable." How do they begin to feel they're welcomed, they belong, they're part of what's happening here?
- **Commitment.** "I'm part of it." What specific decision confirms that they're part of the family?
- **Maturation.** "I'm growing." It's not enough that they have joined us. How do we help them develop their faith in Christ?
- **Ministry.** "I'm serving." What are the ways we help them serve the Lord and serve each other?
- **Multiplication.** "I'm reproducing." How do we encourage them to influence others for Christ's sake?

Evaluate your existing Programs and ministries in light of these steps you have established. List these Programs on a chart. Where are the gaps? Where are the overlaps? Where are the bridges between each of the steps? Where are the barriers? Evaluate how much of your financial resource is allocated for each part of this People Process. Evaluate how many people—your human resources in the church—are involved in each phase. God has promised you wisdom and guidance. *"I guide you in the way of wisdom and lead you along straight paths."* (Prov. 4:11)

Peter quoted David from Ps. 16:11, on the day of Pentecost, when the Church was born. *"'You have made known to me the paths of life; you will fill me with joy in your presence.'"* (Acts 2:28)

Make the Pathway clear so that people can be healthy, growing, purposeful believers!

15

PASS IT ON

"Shoelaces and Rubber Bands"

Jesus prayerfully and carefully chose his twelve disciples. I wonder how frustrated he became with them at times. After Peter made his insightful declaration, *"You are the Christ, the Son of the living God"* (Matt. 16:16), Jesus had made his first pronouncement about building his Church and using Peter to do it. But the Lord had to rebuke him; *"Get behind me, Satan! You are a stumbling block to me; you do not have in mind the things of God, but the things of men."* (Matt. 16:23)

What a disappointment. Peter became an obstacle rather than a vehicle. Tell me, would you have trusted Jesus' disciples with your mission?!

A. Christ's Last Night with His Disciples

He reaffirmed primary principles. In John 13 and 14, Jesus gave the disciples the ultimate serving lesson by washing their feet; he encouraged them to love one another, told them he was the way, the truth and the life, promised them his peace, and reaffirmed that he was coming back.

He restated his vision. In John 15, he told the disciples to draw their life from him, and to bear much fruit.

He released the ministry to them. He reminded them that he had chosen and appointed them (John 15:16), and that he was conferring on them his Kingdom. (Luke 22:28)

On their last night together, as they shared the Last Supper, Jesus expressed his mandate for them: *"A new command I give you: Love one another. As I have loved you, so you must love one another. By this all men will know that you are my disciples, if you love one another."* (John 13:34) The disciples were still having trouble with their hearing: Luke tells us (22:24) that they were preoccupied with their significance rather than his; arguing about who was most important rather than recognizing Christ's preeminence. Their arguing was followed by Judas' departure and betrayal, and Jesus' recognition of Peter's impending denial.

I wonder how Jesus felt. He expressed hope regarding his disciples as leaders, while they were acting like turkeys! Most amazing about that night is that Christ passed the baton to them; he affirmed them for standing by him, and he conferred on them his Kingdom. (Luke 22:28-31) He even said to Peter, *"when you have turned back, strengthen your brothers."* (v. 32)

Who are we to think that there are foolproof processes for developing leaders, or that we won't have significant disappointments at strategic times? In spite of questions that night, Jesus still passed the baton on to the disciples and entrusted them with his first love, the Church.

B. Leaders, Remember Your Primary Tasks:

Reaffirm primary principles – *Teach.* With the authority of God's Word, we must speak God's truth with love: where else will people hear it in our world? The fundamental principles of the Church bear repeating often. A primary task of the leader is to keep assumptions clear; to see that the foundations on which the church is built are continually communicated. I've learned a lesson about leadership: don't presume that the assumptions of the church are passed on by osmosis. I found myself assuming that because I had articulated leadership principles and the basic foundational concepts of Calvary Community, that they were understood by everyone on the staff and most of the church body. False assumption.

Restate the vision – *Lead.* We are the keepers and communicators of the vision. The leader must keep that vision fresh and clear. Is there anything more frustrating than watching a movie when the picture is out of focus? I recall sitting in a theater for 2 or 3 minutes with an out-of-focus picture. The irritation began to build, and the murmuring in the theater grew exponentially. Finally, I got up, went out and talked to the management. The cameraman was obviously not watching the screen. The projector was working, but the focus wasn't clear. A primary task of the leader is not just to see that the camera is running, but to see that the vision stays in focus. The Purpose doesn't change, but the vision needs to be restated periodically. At Calvary, we eventually went through a re-visioning process—to give fresh, contemporary focus to our mission.

RUBBER BANDS. Ever take one end of a rubber band and pull on it while someone is holding the other end? The more you pull, the higher the tension, the anxiety. Pull it too hard—it snaps—and everyone gets stung. Leadership is knowing how much tension to put on the rubber band. When there is no tension, People aren't challenged to leave their comfort zones and reach for God's Purpose. When the leader pulls too far—snap!—everyone gets hurt.

Release ministry to others – *Equip*. Bottlenecks are always at the top. Many churches are limited in their ministry to the personal capacity of the top—the pastor. Leaders/pastors are often bottlenecks. We must give ministry away, even if we aren't convinced our people are ready.

TIE SHOELACES. A principle of leadership is learning to tie shoelaces. Tie the person with a need to a person who can help. Take literally the words of 2 Corinthians 1:3-5:

> *"Praise be to the God and Father of our Lord Jesus Christ, the Father of compassion and the God of all comfort, who comforts us in all our troubles, so that we can comfort those in any trouble with the comfort we ourselves have received from God. For just as the sufferings of Christ flow over into our lives, so also through Christ our comfort overflows."*

Let people do it! Frequently, as I'm outside, greeting people following a Celebration, needs come up or someone mentions a concern. I quickly look around and pray, "Lord, who is there here right now who can relate to this need and can help?" It's amazing how often God gives opportunities to tie shoelaces, if you're looking for them. Where is the person with a need? Who can help meet that need?

"Joe, this is John. He'd like to know more about how to make a personal commitment to Christ. Could you two get together and talk about it?" Don't hoard the blessings—tie the shoelaces, and then move away and allow the people in the body to minister to each other and receive the blessing.

C. Paul's Parting Words to Timothy

Be there for the long haul. After serving for many years in the work of the Lord, Paul was concerned that he would not be cast away or lose his integrity as a leader. These are nearly the last words in the last book Paul wrote, as he considered his life in retrospect. He looked back and simply said:

> *"I have fought the good fight,"*—I've competed well
>
> *"I have finished the race,"*—I've completed the course
>
> *"I have kept the faith."*—I've kept the rules. (2 Tim. 4:7)

Fight the good fight. It is a fight, but it's a good fight. It's a fight that demands your all, if you're a committed leader. But expect to win. The victory is the Lord's.

It's a marathon. The work of being a spiritual leader is not a dash; it's a marathon, and pacing is important. When the Greeks defeated the Persians in the Battle of Marathon, a soldier ran all the way back to Greece. Totally exhausted, he exclaimed, "Rejoice! We've conquered!" Then he collapsed and died. That's the origin of the marathon. Plan to finish the race.

Keep the faith. I think this means to live by the rules; hold on to the essentials, the truth of the Word of God. Fear God more than you fear people What's important? The fact is, not much! But hold on to what is important—keeping faith in God.

Mark some milestones. As God gives victories, and as major accomplishments take place, mark and record them. Give credit to God for them. Share them and celebrate them with the congregation.

Mind the finish line. Sometimes when running a marathon in a valley, the finish line isn't even visible, but it had better be visible in the mind of the runner. Paul spoke to Timothy about *"that day."* (2 Tim. 4:8) It was visible in Paul's mind as he looked back and as he looked forward, toward his finish line.

The Big Day is coming. Paul was saying he was longing for it. He knew the Judge was going to pass out the awards—the crown of righteousness to everyone who finished the race. Paul was committed to being there and finishing the course.

As I observe pastors, one of my prayers is that we will run the race with integrity, that we'll fight the good fight, and that God will give us finishing wisdom and grace. Jesus understood the necessity of being alone with his Father regularly. Healthy pacing means time alone with God on a daily basis. For Paul and for us—we will never have the Emperor place a laurel wreath on our heads for winning the Marathon. But we will receive a crown of righteousness from the Lord of the universe on that Great Day.

The Big Day is coming!

> *"Now there is in store/or me the crown of righteousness, which the Lord, the righteous Judge, will award me on that day—and not only to me, but also to all who have longed for his appearing."* (2 Tim. 4:8)

CONCLUSION

PLACE CONFIDENCE FOR THE FUTURE IN CHRIST

A. The Best is Yet to Come

Encourage people; but place *your* confidence in Christ. Frequently, I see pastors who have lost confidence about the future because they are looking at people. People are not an acceptable foundation for our confidence, anyway. Our certainty has to come from the Lord. I assume we all go through times when our self-confidence wanes. That's the struggle for every 5-year-old as he first goes off to school, every teenager as he walks onto a high school campus, every pastor as he starts his first work. I looked back at the five-year mark and the fifteen-year mark, and I had doubts and questions about my capacity to continue as the leader at Calvary Community. Our confidence is in the Lord who made heaven and earth, not in people, not in our own abilities.

The best is yet to come! One of Christ's most amazing statements was made at the final dinner with his disciples: "*I tell you the truth, anyone who has faith in me will do what I have been doing. He will do even greater things than these, because I am going to the Father.*" (John 14:12)

Christ encouraged the disciples to claim greater days through the greater power . . . the personal power of the Holy Spirit, whom he talked about next. (John 14:16ff.) Assume that there are greater days ahead!

B. The Harvest is Ready—Now!

The disciples were busy with maintenance ministry; they had gone to buy lunch. They were probably thinking, ***Someday Christ's Kingdom will happen;*** and, ***Much more will happen when we assume what Jesus talked about in John 4:35***: *"Do you not say, 'Four months more and then the harvest'? I tell you, open your eyes and look at the fields! They are ripe for harvest."*

Make the assumption that the harvest is ready—now! And make the assumption that the harvest is plentiful! *"The harvest is plentiful but the workers are few."* (Matt. 9:37) There are more people ready to respond to the Good News than there are workers ready to share it in life terms they can understand.

- There is a lot of ripened fruit—**now**
- God is at work to bring people to himself—**now**
- People need to hear the Gospel in terms they can understand – **now**

C. Christ is This World's Last Hope!

Peter Drucker has said, "The last great hope for America is the Church."

Someday heaven's Grand Opening is going to happen.

Date T.B.A. (to be announced)

We're all invited. I can't wait!

We're here now to pass out the Invitations!

WE WAIT FOR THE *blessed hope*
—THE *glorious* APPEARING OF
OUR GREAT GOD AND *Savior*
Jesus Christ.

— TITUS 2:13

Made in the USA
Las Vegas, NV
08 March 2024